LYDIA, WIFE OF HUGH MILLER OF CROMARTY

# LYDIA

## Wife of Hugh Miller
## of Cromarty

Elizabeth Sutherland
in co-operation with Lydia's
great-great-granddaughter
Marian McKenzie Johnston

TUCKWELL PRESS

First published in Great Britain in 2002 by
Tuckwell Press Ltd
The Mill House, Phantassie
East Linton, East Lothian, Scotland
Reprinted 2003
Copyright © Elizabeth Sutherland 2002
Foreword copyright © Lord Mackay of Clashfern
Introduction copyright © Marian McKenzie Johnston

ISBN 1 86232 221 X

*British Library Cataloguing-in-Publication Data*
A catalogue record is available on request
from the British Library

Typeset by Antony Gray
Printed and bound by Bell and Bain Ltd, Glasgow

# Contents

# List of illustrations

# Foreword

BY LORD MACKAY OF CLASHFERN

It will be two hundred years on 10th October 2002 since Hugh Miller was born in Cromarty, and he still exerts a fascination on account of his remarkable achievements. With his school days ending rather abruptly and his formal education being consequently incomplete, he nevertheless succeeded in reaching great success as a writer and as an authority on geology recognised by the leading men of his time. The sad circumstances of his death at the age of fifty-four add a poignancy to his memory. That he was able to do so much while having earned his living at the beginning of his working life as a stonemason is an enigma which still arouses considerable interest.

After a courtship and engagement of some three years Hugh married Lydia Fraser in Cromarty on 7th January 1837. During their marriage, they attained great prominence as a result of Hugh becoming the editor of *The Witness* and the family moving to Edinburgh in 1840. Although by no means only a religious paper, *The Witness* was at the centre of the controversy which rent the Church of Scotland in the early part of the nineteenth century, culminating in the Disruption in 1843 when church affairs were at the very centre of Scottish public life. It was natural therefore that enormous interest was taken in and strong feelings were aroused by the editor of this central voice in the controversy. His tragic death at his own hand, along with the great variety of his literary and scientific works, has served to maintain this interest to the present time.

But what of Lydia, his wife of some twenty years, and his widow for almost as long? This account by Elizabeth Sutherland with co-operation from the Millers' great-great-granddaughter, Marian McKenzie Johnston, is as full an answer to that question as the available information can produce. Careful scrutiny of public sources and the extant private records and correspondence have been skilfully used by the well-known author to build up an impressive picture of Lydia's part in the couple's marriage, and of the superhuman effort she undertook in publishing so much of what Hugh had left written but unpublished at his death. Plagued by ill health, and of a somewhat nervous and restless disposition, Lydia managed to secure very distinguished help in this work, and although not a scientist herself managed to carry it out to a high standard of accuracy which has greatly enhanced the legacy Hugh has left to the world, over what it would have been had nothing been published after his death. Apart from this, Lydia is shown as a person of great natural talent who produced one rather polemical style of novel and was a successful writer of books for children whose influence on the quality of Hugh's work was considerable. Along with the account of the sad death of their first child 'Little Eliza', whose tombstone Hugh lovingly carved, the account of the couple's surviving children adds a valuable complement to what we already know about the Millers' life which is specially welcome in this the 200th anniversary of Hugh's birth. The power of religion in family life in the era in which the Millers lived is captured in quotations from Lydia's writing which at the same time reflect her enthusiasm for teaching, her skill at it, and her love for children. To those who wish to understand the spirit that inspired the Scottish people in the middle of the nineteenth century this intimate account of Lydia's life will make a valuable contribution.

# Introduction

BY MARIAN McKENZIE JOHNSTON

Hugh and Lydia Miller had five children, one of whom died young. The four who survived were Harriet (Davidson), William, Bessie (Mackay) and Hugh junior. My grandmother, Lydia Davidson Middleton, with whom I stayed often as a child, was Harriet's eldest daughter. She and Tom Middleton had two children, my father Alastair and my Aunt Margaret, who never married. In 1980 at the age of 85 Aunt Margaret, because of failing eyesight, had to move into a Residential Home. Her house was sold and she told me to take the family papers – in two trunks and several boxes and bags. Unfortunately a burglar some years before had found them and tipped the contents onto the floor. The elastic bands holding the bundles of letters had broken and everything had been put back in a muddle, including unsorted letters dating from 1797 to 1943, many undated. As I worked through these I read them to my Aunt, who identified and described some of the people mentioned.

One letter was from my grandmother Lydia to her youngest sister Harriet Felkin in New Zealand in 1934, saying she had written to her cousin Hugh Mackay to ask if he could find any of her mother Harriet's letters. He had replied that Bessie 'had amassed trunks and trunks of family papers and correspondence' and that it was 'too difficult' to go through them. However, his young daughter Betty made a search and sent my grandmother a small and random collection, mostly from Harriet Davidson to her mother, but also some from the other Miller children. There were a few from Lydia Miller herself but only one of any real interest.

Another letter was from my grandfather, Tom Middleton, then Professor of Agriculture employed by the Gackwar of Baroda in India (at 550 Rupees a month), written on 26 January 1890 to his future wife. On his engagement to my grandmother he had been presented by Hugh junior with a complete set of Hugh Miller's published works (which I now have) and he wrote: 'I have been looking over one of your grandfather's books today and read a good bit of the Preface by Lydia. Your grandmother must have studied geology pretty closely, for her Preface to these lectures on geology shows she was well up in the history and literature of the science. Some of the conclusions of her sentences, however, are very woman-ish, the triumphant way in which she disposes of her opponents' arguments for example'.

In his *My Schools and Schoolmasters* Hugh Miller drew a picture of Lydia as a young girl. She collaborated with Peter Bayne in writing his *Life and Letters of Hugh Miller* and appears in the background. By the time I had got Harriet's letters in as near chronological order as possible, using mentions of births of children and what flowers were out in the garden as the main clues, I had a fair idea of the characters of the four Miller children. They all frequently referred to the 'long and interesting' or 'long and kind' letters from their mother. But where were these, and what was this older Lydia like herself?

About 1990 I found that the Miller genealogical chart in the Hugh Miller Cottage in Cromarty had disappeared and decided to attempt a reconstruction of both ascendants and descendants of Hugh and Lydia. With the help of the Cottage visitors' book I found Bessie's granddaughter Ann (Mackay) Rider, who provided some papers and books and a lot of answers. Ann knew that her mother Irene had been with Lydia Mackay when she died, and that the 'trunks and trunks' had been inherited by brother Hugh, whose home in Brighton had received a direct hit from a German bomb in the Second World War. So no hope of getting sight of all the missing letters.

'Looking for Lydia' seemed like trying to complete a thousand-piece jigsaw puzzle with most of the pieces missing. Some of these have been found on gravestones and in old parish records, wills, sasines (land records), census records, street directories, death cer-tificates etc. Katherine Cameron undertook the task of trawling through microfiches of the Northern newspapers of the time. Dr Michael Taylor has provided a great deal of information. None of my Miller family letters records important events such as the publication of Lydia's books for children or her novel. She had been thought worthy of an entry in the *Dictionary of National Biography*, but still the persona was absent.

I know from Harriet's letters and personal knowledge of my grandmother and my aunt that they all inherited Lydia's literary and musical talents, found domestic duties 'tedious' but performed them conscientiously, were keen gardeners, always had beautifully arranged flowers in the house and were exceptionally 'good with the needle' (my grandmother taught me to darn and patch as well as knit and dress-make and embroider from the age of six). I can hear Lydia's sighs when Hugh returned from his geologising trips with his 'russet suit' frayed and torn. (Unpicking and 'contriving' to rearrange worn trouser bottoms, and mending pockets, were my least favourite jobs when newly married just after the Second World War.)

I was told from an early age that I should be the fifth generation of women writers in the family, but alas I am not. Which is why I invited our friend Elizabeth Sutherland, a professional writer who lives in the Black Isle and knows its history, to write the story of Lydia. There are still many gaps, but she has skilfully pulled together such strands as we could find. There is little in surviving papers to reveal Lydia's own opinions and feelings. But the fact that she so successfully completed her self-imposed task after Hugh's suicide of ensuring that his writings were kept before the public is evidence of her own strength of character and belief in her husband's work.

# Acknowledgements

I owe thanks to many individuals and institutions who have contributed in various ways to the writing of this book, including living descendants of Hugh and Lydia Miller. Chief among the latter has been their great-great-granddaughter, Marian McKenzie Johnston, who invited me to write this biography and has done much of the research, as well as lending me her family papers. I am very grateful to her, and to her husband Henry who has spent many hours editing and preparing the typescript through countless changes.

Marian and I wish to make special mention of Dr Michael Taylor, Curator of Vertebrate Palaeontology at the National Museums of Scotland, and Katherine Cameron of Inverness, both of whom have devoted much time to helping with research and offering comments. The latter in particular has been indefatigable in trying, alas in the end without success, to identify Lydia's father, William Fraser. We are also greatly indebted to Frieda Gostwick, Manager of the Hugh Miller Cottage in Cromarty, her husband Martin, writer and journalist, and Dr David Alston, Curator of Cromarty Courthouse, who have been unstinting in helping in research, in offering helpful suggestions and advice, and generally providing enthusiastic encouragement.

Other individuals who have readily helped include Dr Margaret Allen of the Department of Social Inquiry, Adelaide University; David Bowcock of the Archives Service of Cumbria County Council; David Fowler of the Stornoway Public Library; Cyril Greenslade of the Egham Historical Society; Alison Lindsay of the National Archives of Scotland; Iain Maciver and Sheila Mackenzie of the National Library of Scotland; Helen Peden of the British Library; Mr N M Plumley, Curator of Christ's Hospital Museum; Harald Salvesen of Norway; Patrick Simpson of Edinburgh; Richard Smout,

Isle of Wight County Archivist; Sara Stevenson of the Scottish National Portrait Gallery.

We are indebted to the staff of Inverness Museum for their ever willing cooperation. Dingwall and Inverness Public Libraries have also been most helpful, particularly Alistair Macleod of the latter, and also the Archivist of the Society of Jesus in London. Special thanks are due to Morag Williams of the Dumfries and Galloway Health Board for her help, particularly in locating Lydia's medical case notes held in the archives of Crichton Royal Hospital lodged in the Crichton Royal Museum and giving permission to quote from them; and to both Alistair Tough and Karl Magee for similar help and permission to quote from the records relevant to Lydia's stay in the Gartnavel Asylum held in the Greater Glasgow Health Board Archive under reference HB 13/7/72.

# Chronology

1802 Hugh Miller born 10 October

1812 Lydia Falconer Fraser baptised 25 January

1822 Thomas Mackenzie Fraser, Lydia's brother, baptised
15 August

1827 Lydia goes to Edinburgh, probably about October

1828 Lydia's father dies 10 June

1829 Thomas enters Christ's Hospital school 3 April
Lydia goes to stay with relations in Egham, Surrey

1830 Lydia joins her mother in Cromarty

1831 Lydia's first sight of Hugh, June

1833 Lydia falls in love with Hugh, late summer
They become engaged, November

1834 Hugh given a post in the Commercial Bank in Cromarty,
November

1835 Lydia's portrait painted by Grigor Urquhart
Hugh's *Scenes and Legends of the North of Scotland* published

1837 Marriage of Hugh and Lydia in Cromarty 7 January
Birth of Elizabeth Logan Miller ('little Eliza') 23 November

1839 Death of 'little Eliza' 25 August
Birth of Harriet Miller 25 November

1840 Hugh takes up his appointment as editor of *The Witness* in
Edinburgh, January
Lydia and family join Hugh in Edinburgh, Spring

1841 Hugh's *The Old Red Sandstone* published

1842 William Miller born 28 October

1843  The 'Disruption' of the Church of Scotland 18 May

1845  Elizabeth ('Bessie') Miller born 19 June

1846  First of Lydia's books for children published under the pseudonym Mrs Myrtle

1847  Lydia's novel *Passages in the Life of an English Heiress* published anonymously
Hugh's *First Impressions of England and Its People* published

1849  Lydia's brother Thomas marries Caroline Neale

1850  Hugh Miller II born 15 July

1854  Hugh buys the house Shrub Mount, Portobello, April

1856  Hugh dies at Shrub Mount 26 December

1857  Hugh's *Testimony of the Rocks* published posthumously by Lydia
Lydia goes to Malvern for a 'cure', April
Hugh's *The Cruise of the Betsey* published posthumously with Preface by the Reverend W. S. Symonds

1858  Lydia returns to Edinburgh, 27 Ann Street, May
Lydia's Preface to Hugh's posthumous *Sketch-book of Popular Geology*, October

1860  Move to 19 Regent Terrace, Edinburgh, Spring
Lydia's Preface to new edition of Hugh's *Footprints of the Creator* published
Family holiday in Germany, Summer

1861  Lydia goes to stay with the Nobles near Poolewe, August

1862  Lydia returns to Edinburgh, May
Lydia and young Hugh take short holiday in France, September
Lydia's Preface to Hugh's posthumous *Tales and Sketches* 23 December
Lydia helping Peter Bayne to produce Hugh's posthumous *Essays*

1863  Harriet marries John Davidson 14 April
Lydia's Preface to Hugh's posthumous *Edinburgh and its Neighbourhood*

Lydia admitted to Crichton Royal Institution, Dumfries 10 October until 13 November

1865 Lydia's 'cure' at Milnethorpe, Westmorland, May
Lydia admitted to Glasgow Royal Asylum 20 June until 21 July
Lydia's mother dies 18 August

1867 Lydia admitted to Crichton Royal Institution 28 December until 1 May 1868

1870 Harriet and John Davidson go to Australia, March

1871 Bayne's *Life and Letters of Hugh Miller* published

1872 'Bessie' marries Norman Mackay 2 July
William marries 'Maggie' Sutherland, September

1875 Lydia goes to stay with Bessie and Norman Mackay at Assynt, May

1876 Lydia dies at Assynt 11 March

1878 Lydia's son Hugh marries Jeannie Morison Campbell

# SIMPLIFIED GENEALOGY
*(showing living descendants underlined)*

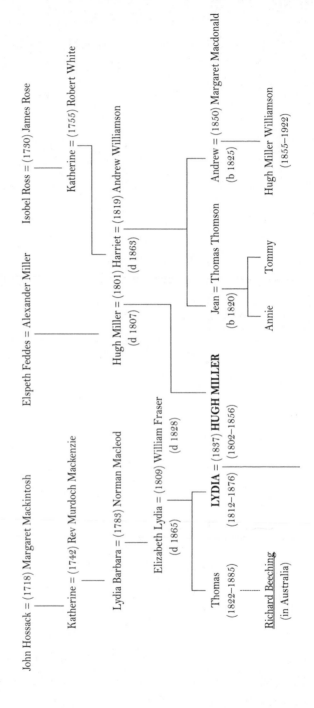

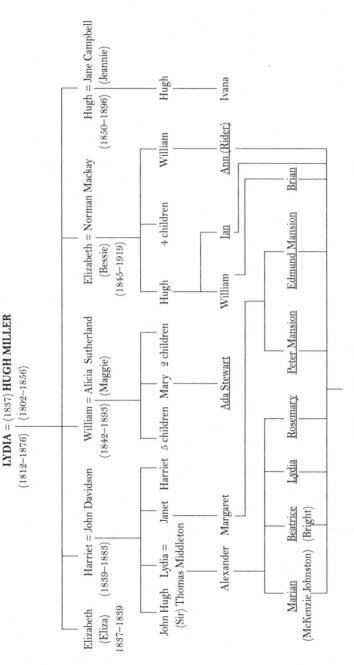

**LYDIA** = (1837) **HUGH MILLER**
(1812–1876)    (1802–1856)

Elizabeth (Eliza) 1837–1839

Harriet = John Davidson (1839–1883)

William = Alicia Sutherland (1842–1893) (Maggie)

Elizabeth = Norman Mackay (Bessie) (1845–1919)

Hugh = Jane Campbell (1850–1896) (Jeannie)

John Hugh   Lydia = (Sir) Thomas Middleton   Janet   Harriet   5 children   Mary   2 children

Hugh   4 children   William

Hugh   Ivana

Alexander   Margaret

Ada Stewart

William   Ian   Ann (Rider)

Marian (McKenzie Johnston)   Beatrice (Bright)   Lydia   Rosemary

Peter Mansion   Edmund Mansion   Brian

57 children and grandchildren

# ONE

# An Unlikely Pair

Young Lydia Fraser was feeling listless and weary 'late on the evening of a very hot summer Sabbath' in 1833. In the still and sultry gloaming, not intending to walk anywhere, she slipped out of her widowed mother's house, Braefoot Cottage on Church Street in the small coastal town of Cromarty, to listen to 'the murmur of the sea, whose waves beat on the nearby shore'. However, seeking a cooling breeze, she climbed the path to the ancient, ruined Chapel of St Regulus. Here she could look through the trees across the Cromarty Firth towards distant Ben Wyvis, slowly fading from view in the darkening western sky as the first stars became visible above her. Deep in thought, she was suddenly startled to find Hugh Miller standing beside her. It was an awkward meeting, for a few months earlier her mother, fearing she was falling in love with a man she thought unsuitable as a husband, had forbidden her to see him, an edict they had both tried to obey. Hugh acted honourably. Simply remarking on the sweetness of the evening and the view, politely but without feeling, he quickly resumed his walk. Lydia, however, who had previously not thought of him as a prospective husband, only a very good friend with whom she could discuss serious matters of religion and philosophy, experienced a sudden leap of the heart – and realised she was in love. She then, as she put it in her Memoir written years later, 'knelt at a cold gravestone and registered over the dead a vow, rash and foolish perhaps, but it was kept'. The first step into a romantic but ultimately tragic marriage had been taken.

\*     \*     \*

Mrs Fraser's attitude towards her daughter's friendship with Hugh Miller was understandable. To all outward appearances they were an ill-assorted pair. Lydia, aged twenty-one, slight, pretty and well educated – Hugh, ten years older, nearly six feet in height, a broad-chested giant in comparison, his face ruggedly chiselled, his school education uncompleted, and working as a simple stonemason. In reality they were a well-matched couple, the qualities of the one complementing those of the other. And Hugh had long realised that he was deeply in love with Lydia. It was not that Mrs Fraser thought badly of him as a man. Indeed, in common with most of Cromarty she admired his personality and intellect. Three years earlier she had written to Lydia, then in England, commenting favourably on this unusual man. But he had no steady income and apparently had little intention of settling down to earn one. She wanted more security for her daughter.

Hugh had been born in Cromarty on 10 October, 1802, the eldest child of another Hugh Miller and his wife Harriet Wright, whose father had been a Cromarty shoemaker. Hugh senior, a widower of forty-seven when he married Harriet aged twenty-one, came from a long line of seafarers and was a man of substance in such a small place, captain of his own trading schooner. But he was drowned when his ship sank in a storm in 1807. It was many years before even a fraction of its value could be realised from the insurance cover. His widow was left to bring up a five-year-old boy and his two younger sisters in the cottage of six small rooms built by her husband's buccaneering grandfather over a hundred years before. Fortunately her two unmarried brothers, James and Sandy Wright, who lived nearby, both earned modest incomes.

James was a saddler and Sandy, who, according to Hugh's auto-biography *My Schools and Schoolmasters*, had 'sailed with Nelson' in the Napoleonic wars, had turned from his original trade of cartwright to that of sawyer. They helped their sister financially as much as they could but, more importantly, they devoted themselves to young Hugh's intellectual development. Although only working men with little formal education, they had fine enquiring minds, possessed a library of some one hundred and fifty books, were wise in life's ways and were devout Presbyterians.

Under the guidance of his uncles Hugh became an avid reader.

Hugh considered he 'owed to them much more of my real education than to any of the teachers whose schools I afterwards attended'. From James he gained his first interest in the legends and lore of the North. By Sandy he was introduced to the natural history and rocks of the immediate neighbourhood and taught the importance of close observation.

Formal schooling, however, was another matter. Bored and irritated by what he regarded as pedantic teaching at the local parish school and later the grammar school, Hugh took to playing truant. He became leader of a gang of like-minded boys who would spend days and even nights in adventures among the caves and cliffs along the coast. Finally, when he was fifteen, he had a dispute with his English master leading to a physical brawl and the end of his schooldays. Then, in 1819, his two sisters having died in quick succession of some fever in 1816, his mother re-married, against the opposition of her two brothers and Hugh's disapproval. The following year Hugh, disregarding his uncles' urging to go to university, for which they were prepared to pay, decided to become a stonemason.

As a young boy Hugh had been taken by his mother to stay with her eldest sister Isobel (twenty-four years her senior) who was married to George Munro, factor to the Barony of Gruids in Sutherland. George's youngest son, another George, was a mason, and Hugh envied his 'long winter holidays, and how delightfully he employed them'. So, rather than seek all-the-year-round work, he apprenticed himself to the husband of another of his mother's sisters, David Williamson, also a mason, judging that he would thus have time during the winter to pursue his interest in literature and the natural sciences.

Although Hugh earned little money as a stonemason during the next three years, and damaged his physical health permanently by contracting a lung ailment from his stonecutting work, he gained much from it in other ways. As he travelled the countryside as a journeyman mason, living in the harshest conditions, he read a lot and had opportunities to study the strata and rocks with which he was working and to uncover fossils which fascinated him. He learned to admire the characters of the best of his fellow workers and to have contempt for the attitude of some of the 'gentry' towards them. While working at Niddrie, south of Edinburgh (a developing city which he explored with admiring wonder), however, he learned to distrust the depraved urban workers and detest the radical and Chartist agitators among them, even though he understood the causes of their unrest and bitterness. All this experience of humanity played its part in developing his attitudes to social questions in later years.

When his health broke down completely in 1824, in his twenty-second year, Hugh returned to Cromarty to recover under the care of his mother, who now had a new family of two little girls (a boy was born the following year). Once able to work again, he began to use his well-developed stonecutting skills and naturally artistic eye to earn a few shillings locally by sculpting and inscribing tombstones. He even built a simple stone one-roomed house for his destitute aunt Jenny. But his greatest pleasure came from pursuing his now eager interest in geology and fossils, which was to lead him into correspondence and personal contact with distinguished professional and amateur geologists and zoologists. He also renewed his friendship with John Swanson, who had been one of his fellow adventurers in his schooldays (but, unlike him, a conscientious scholar) and was now training for the ministry at King's College, Aberdeen. Under his influence, and even more so that of Cromarty's inspiring Minister, the Reverend Alexander Stewart, he began to develop the evangelical Presbyterianism which was to become such an important part of his life.

During his schooldays, Hugh had shown considerable skill as a storyteller, and had enjoyed versifying. While working as a stone-mason, he had often composed poems around his experiences which expressed his feeling for scenery and nature. He failed to persuade Robert Carruthers, editor of the *Inverness Courier,* to publish a slim volume of these, and produced it at his own expense in 1829. They were not very good, as Carruthers had recognised, and they re-ceived a lukewarm public response. But Carruthers realised Hugh could write prose of high quality and printed in the paper his five *Letters on the Herring Fishery* describing his experiences when out with the fishing fleet and the lives of the fishermen. The style and content caught the public's attention. They were re-published as a pamphlet and almost overnight Hugh's name became widely known throughout Scotland – it is said that no less a man than Walter Scott scrambled for a copy. In addition he uncovered some hitherto unknown fossil fishes which made his name amongst leading zoologists and palaeontologists.

Hugh, however, had a profound distrust of patronage and declined to take up the possibility of turning to a professional literary career with the help of well-wishers. His material wants being few, he preferred to remain quietly in Cromarty, stonecutting and carving as his fancy took him and commissions offered, pursuing his fossil hunting – and writing. In that small (2215 inhabitants in 1831) egalitarian society, where a man was 'a man for a' that', this 'stonemason poet', with his natural, gentle courtesy and ability by then, despite his lack of formal education, to join in a wide range of intellectual discussions, was a welcome guest in any parlour. He became a 'lion', not patronised, but admired as a son of Cromarty to be proud of.

\*     \*     \*

Lydia Falconer Fraser, baptised in Inverness on 25 January, 1812, had had a very different upbringing. Her mother, Elizabeth Lydia Macleod, was the granddaughter of the Reverend Murdoch Mackenzie (described by Elizabeth as 'younger of Redcastle', an ancient barony with a line stretching back to the Mackenzies of Kintail). His wife was the daughter of John Hossack, four times Provost of Inverness,[1] married to Margaret Macintosh, a daughter of the barony of Termit. There were connections too with the Cuthberts of Castlehill, Davidsons, Macdonalds and Falconers. In common with most families in the north of Scotland at that time, this lineage, this

---

1 John Hossack was Provost in 1735–38, 1741–44, 1753–56 and 1758–61. As a close friend of Duncan Forbes, President of the Court of Session, who was loyal to King George at the time of the Jacobite uprising in 1745, he tried unsuccessfully to intervene with the Duke of Cumberland on behalf of the defeated Jacobite militia after the Battle of Culloden.

'silver thread of high descent' as Hugh Miller later put it in his story of William Forsyth included in his posthumous *Tales and Sketches,* was a matter of great pride for Elizabeth, and never forgotten by Lydia. Hugh, through his mother, could also have traced his ancestry back to the Mackenzies of Kintail. But it was his lack of income and apparent lack of prospects that influenced Elizabeth, for she herself had experienced poverty and wanted none of it for her daughter. Her father, Norman Macleod, had made money in Jamaica but had lost it in unwise ventures on his return to Scotland; and her husband had failed in business.

Elizabeth had married, in 1809 at the age of twenty-one, a William Fraser of whose background nothing is known for certain. If his age at his death on 10 June 1828 was correctly recorded as thirty-nine on the family memorial stone in the Chapel Burial Ground in Inverness, he must have been her age when they married, possibly even slightly younger, which was unusual in those days. Extensive research has failed to turn up either a definite identification of this William Fraser or details (or even confirmation) of his apparently early death. In Peter Bayne's *Life and Letters of Hugh Miller* (published in 1871) he is referred to as having been 'notably handsome in youth, and famous in Strathnairn as a deer-stalker' who 'entered, later in life, into business in Inverness, and was at first prosperous, but, being generous and unsuspecting to a fault, was robbed by a clerk and beguiled by a relative, and at last overborne by disappointments and difficulties'. However, in the Register of Deaths the entry for Lydia gives her father's occupation as 'leather worker'. An elderly resident of Inverness has claimed that his uncle told him that his great-great-grandfather, Donald Fraser, had been the illegitimate son of Thomas Fraser of Glenurquhart and half-brother to Hugh Miller's wife's father. If the mason carving thirty-nine on the memorial stone had misread fifty-nine, Lydia's father could have been this William. But there is nothing in the published Fraser pedigree to confirm this claim. There is much to choose from, but nothing to help make a decision. Even the reference to him, in the notice of his widow's death, as 'of Baachan and Inverness' has led nowhere.

Although it has proved impossible to establish the origins and identity of Lydia's father, there seems no reason to doubt that he did become a small merchant with a shop in East (now Church) Street in Inverness (later to become Mackay's bookshop) selling tobacco, snuff and liquor, and leather goods, and that his business failed. In Inverness in those days, with a population of less than twelve thousand, social structure was flexible and (according to Isabel Harriet Anderson's *Inverness before the Railways*, published in 1885) a 'sympathy and freedom from rivalry' existed between social classes. Wealth as such was 'held in small estimation', the leaders of society enjoying in fact only moderate incomes. 'Lawyers and bankers lived mostly in plainly furnished houses above their banks and offices, and shop-keepers in still plainer houses above their shops'. According to George Cameron (*A History and Description of the Town of Inverness*, published in 1846), virtually the only private carriages to be seen in town were those bringing the country gentry to church on Sunday, and there were only two simple carriages ('noddies') for hire. Men servants were almost unknown.

Lydia in her early childhood, therefore, would probably have been unaware of any significant financial gulf between her parents and the rest of society, even when her father's business began to run into difficulties. Children went to parties in each other's homes more or less regardless of their parents' circumstances, dressed in nothing finer than their Sunday wear. Hallowe'en and April Fool's Day ('gawking day') were occasions for universal fun. There is a possibility that her mother may have had to supplement the income from the shop by teaching small children at home, but this would have been nothing remarkable in a town where numerous small schools of that kind existed.[2]

When she was about eight years old, Lydia became a pupil at the Inverness Royal Academy, which had replaced the old grammar school in 1792. A high standard of education was provided for some

2 It may have been Lydia's mother who was the Mrs William Fraser living in Church Street who placed notices in the *Inverness Courier* in May 1817 and 1818 thanking her friends for their kind support and announcing that she was continuing to teach English to boys and girls between the ages of four and seven.

two hundred or more pupils by five masters, teaching girls and boys separately. Many distinguished men owed their later prominence to the grounding received there, including a slightly younger contemporary of Lydia's, Edward Strathearn Gordon (Baron Gordon), who became Solicitor General for Scotland in 1866. The fees were some four or five pounds per half-year, but Lydia amply repaid the outlay. Newspaper reports show that at the end of both sessions in 1822 she was 2nd dux in the second class for 'Ladies' in French, taught by a Mr Villemer, who was the author of several books in French and a poem called *Astronomie*, published in 1824; and she was 3rd in arithmetic, taught by Mr John Clark. In 1825 she was 2nd dux in the first class for Italian (also taught by Mr Villemer) and French, and in the second class for geography, taught by the Rector, Mr Adam. She does not appear as a prizewinner during the next two years, but it is likely that she remained at the Academy until the end of the summer session of 1827 when she was fifteen and went to Edinburgh.

One of the unanswered questions in Lydia's life is how much she knew at this time (or even later) of her father's financial troubles – indeed not only that, but just what those troubles involved – or the circumstances of his death. Many years later, when a widow herself, Lydia wrote a Memoir of her life. This, 'somewhat fragmentary and incomplete', came into the possession of her granddaughter, Lydia Miller Mackay, who edited it for publication in *Chambers' Journal* in 1902. The published version begins only when Lydia went to Edinburgh, and nowhere in it, or indeed in any other surviving family papers, is there any mention at all of her father or his family. Was there mention of him in an earlier section later lost, or omitted in the editing? Would details have emerged from the family papers lost in Brighton from enemy bombing during World War II? It is hard to believe, however, that at the age of fifteen, and only a year before his death, Lydia did not have some knowledge of the state of affairs, which had probably been deteriorating for several years. It is significant that, in a Will drawn up in 1821, Thomas Mackenzie (who was then living in England after making money in Jamaica) left his niece, Lydia's mother, £2000 in trust for her children, from which she was to enjoy the income, with the proviso that it should 'not be in any manner subject to the Interference, Debts or Engagements of her present or any future husband'.

There are only two published clues to the nature of William's troubles. Hugh Miller, in his *My Schools and Schoolmasters*, referred to him as a 'worthy man who owing to unwise speculations failed in business'. Peter Bayne, in his *Life and Letters of Hugh Miller*, referred to William as having been 'robbed by a clerk and beguiled by a relative'. In the 1820s there were many business failures in Inverness, some perhaps caused simply by difficult local economic conditions after the Napoleonic wars, the building of the Caledonian Canal and the arrival of the railways (leading to cheaper goods reaching Inverness), others perhaps caused by unwise speculation. It is believed that William was a partner in the firm of Fraser and Ross, the liquidation of which was reported in the local press with an invitation to creditors to make claims on such assets as were available. Such creditors could have included quite modest families who believed that they had somehow been cheated, and rumours of wrongdoing may have been circulating. It is interesting that in one of Lydia's daughter Harriet's novels[3] the heroine's father 'who quite worshipped her' speculated foolishly, fell ill after 'receiving some intelligence from London, and died a few weeks later when his affairs were found to be in the greatest confusion. He had taken shares in ever so many things, and none of his undertakings seemed to have prospered. Everything was swallowed up'. Perhaps Lydia knew exactly what had happened and revealed it to Harriet? If only we could know!

It may be that in 1827 Mrs Fraser (who had received her uncle's legacy in 1822 and therefore had a small income of her own), and perhaps her relatives, felt that it would be better if Lydia were away from Inverness while her father's troubles were a matter of public knowledge, and possibly adverse comment. On the other hand the suggestion may have come for quite other reasons from Mr Keith Thomson, the leading music teacher in Inverness at that time, with whom Lydia was probably having lessons. This 'perfect gentleman

---

3 *Christian Osborne's Friends* by Mrs Harriet Miller Davidson, Edinburgh 1869.

. . . with snow-white hair, a refined face and venerable form', whose 'manner was the personification of courtesy', whose 'patience never failed' (George Cameron, *op cit*), had a half-brother, George, in Edinburgh. Although this George was now seventy, he and his wife took into their home at 140 Princes Street, as boarders, a few 'young ladies' to attend classes in the arts such as music and painting, and learn the social graces of conversation and dancing.[4] Of great importance were the opportunities for their charges to meet representatives of the literati of Edinburgh society of the day.

This period in Lydia's life was a significant step in the development of her cultural interests and enquiring mind that were to captivate Hugh Miller and make her his ideal helpmate.

---

4  George Thomson, 1757–1851, trained for the law in Edinburgh but became senior clerk to the Board of Trustees for the Encouragement of Manufactures in Scotland until his retirement in 1839.

# TWO

# From Child to Adolescent

Lydia would almost certainly have travelled by sea from Inverness to Leith. The surviving parts of her Memoir include no mention of this or, indeed, of her impressions of Edinburgh itself. But the contrast with Inverness must have seemed stark. In Princes Street the traffic, although different, would have been as dense and noisy as it is today – the clang of horses' hooves striking the cobbles, the rattle of carriage wheels, the coarse croak of hackney grooms, the cries of street vendors, the importunings of filthy whey-faced children, the mumblings of drunken beggars, the chatter of elegant women, the earnest conversation of pedants, and, sprinkled among the noisy multi-coloured chattering flock, the black-garbed ministerial crows. When Hugh Miller first saw Edinburgh in 1824 he found two cities, past and present, 'set down side by side, as if for purposes of comparison, with a picturesque valley drawn like a deep score between them, to mark off the line of division ... Of its older proportions I used never to tire: I found I could walk among them as purely for the pleasure which accrued as among the wild and picturesque of nature itself; whereas one visit to the elegant streets and ample squares of the new city always proved sufficient to satisfy; and I certainly never felt the desire to return to any of them to saunter in quest of pleasure along the smooth, well-kept pavements. I, of course, except Princes Street'.

140 Princes Street is almost opposite St John's Episcopal Church, the building of which had been completed by William Burn in 1818. From here in 1827 Lydia would have looked over the 'picturesque valley' to the Castle. To her left, at the foot of the Mound, she would have seen the magnificent new building erected by William Playfair for the Board of Manufactures and Fisheries, now the home of the

Royal Scottish Academy, the construction of which is depicted in a painting by Alexander Nasmyth in 1825.

Lydia's Memoir, however, described not her surroundings but the people she met at the Thomsons, especially Mr Thomson himself, 'a handsome, gentlemanly old man, with silver hair, and wearing gold spectacles' who, when she entered the drawing room on her first evening, 'was sitting reading the paper near a blazing fire [but] rose and placed a chair with the same consideration as though I were a princess'. He 'endeared himself to all the boarders by his unfailing cheerfulness, the politeness and attentions of his manners, and the graceful kindness of his conversation at our social meals'. There was a musical party that first evening. George himself, who had been one of the directors of the first Edinburgh musical festival in 1815, played the violin well and had a passion for music. While forming his collections of Scottish, Welsh and Irish songs, he had persuaded such luminaries as Robert Burns, Walter Scott, Byron and Joanna Baillie[5] to revise the original wording, and composers such as Pleyel, Haydn, Beethoven, Weber and Hummel to write accompaniments for them. He had edited the poems of Anne Grant of Laggan.[6] His son-in-law, George Hogarth (whose daughter married Charles Dickens), was 'a splendid violincellist'.[7] Alexander Ballantyne, brother of James, Walter Scott's publisher, and married to George Thomson's sister, was 'a dark little man, full of fun' and 'an exquisite

5  Joanna Baillie, 1762–1851, Scottish dramatist, was best known for her three volumes of *Plays on the Passions* published between 1798 and 1812, and the three dramas in *Miscellaneous Plays* published in 1836. Her play *De Montfort* was produced at Drury Lane by Roger Kemble and Mrs Siddons in 1800. She also published poems, songs and dramatic ballads.
6  Anne Grant, 1755–1838, was the daughter of Duncan Macvicar and lived between the ages of three and thirteen in the Albany area of America when he was stationed there as an army officer. In 1799 she married an army chaplain in Fort Augustus, who died in 1801, leaving her to bring up eight children on a tiny pension. She became a well-known writer of prose and poetry, and Walter Scott was influential in obtaining an annual pension of £100 for her in her final years.
7  George Hogarth, 1783–1870, Writer to the Signet and associate of Walter Scott and other literary figures, was an amateur 'cello player of distinction, and composer, who later became music critic of the *Daily News* in London.

violin-player'. The second Thomson daughter played the piano well and, 'in a mellow and powerful voice, often gave a Scotch song, out of her father's edition, with great effect'.

Although music and musicians were the chief features of the Thomsons' many social evenings, George was also a lover of painting and literature. 'The dining-room was hung with prints of the best masterpieces of art. The drawing-room contained many gems of paintings – among the rest a lovely little example of Wilkie's 'Auld Robin Gray' and Nasmyth's original portrait of Burns.' Among others who came to the house, Lydia remembered particularly the Reverend John Thomson of Duddington, a well-known landscape painter,[8] and William Tennant, 'a large, red-faced man full of quiet fun', who was professor of oriental languages at St Andrews University and had published, in 1812, the six-canto poem *Anster Fair*.

Mrs Anne Grant of Laggan was another frequent visitor. Her correspondence in *Letters from the Mountains*, published in 1806, and her *Memoirs of an American Lady*, published in 1808, had attracted much attention. Her sympathetic way of writing about simple High-land folk may well have influenced Lydia when she came to write her own novel (Chapter Nine). It was through her that Lydia was introduced to the poems of Joanna Baillie. In her Memoir she recalls this 'very dear old lady' reading a book of these poems. Noticing that the light was poor, she took a candle over to help her. 'She looked up at Mr Thomson,' wrote Lydia, 'saying with her peculiarly sweet smile, "Poetry lighted by one of the Graces!" It might as well, I fancy, have been any one else, but that was the style of them.' And she notes: 'I was a little thing – I suppose small for my age, as they sometimes called me "little Lydia". That was a sort of pet-name not quite *en règle*, for we were, of course, always "missed" '.

Lydia must have been happy with the Thomsons (and was disap-pointed that Hugh, some years later, was unable to call on them when on a visit to Edinburgh); but her surviving Memoir mentions only one of her fellow boarders, 'the youngest of the Misses Innes of

8  John Thomson, 1778–1840, is credited in the *Dictionary of National Biography* with earning at that time some £1800 a year from his painting.

Hermiston', whose name, 'a strange one for a girl', was Gordon
Gordon Innes. 'She was my dearly beloved friend, and my room-
companion for a long time. Full of spirit and energy and gaiety, she
yet would often of a night point to a mark on her breast, which she
said she knew would be fatal. She assured us it was the seal of
consumption. Her brother had borne that mark; her brother had died
of consumption. We tried to reason and to laugh her out of this idea.
Yet it came true. A year or two after her return home, while in the
bloom of early womanhood, and while making preparations for the
Duchess of Sutherland's ball, she sickened and died. She desired my
letters to be buried with her: so I heard.'

The Memoir was written at least thirty years later, so her further
comment reflects not her immediate reaction to this sad news, but
rather her feeling in maturity: 'Alas! Alas! I fear there was little in
them but what was frivolous. May God grant that she and I, in the
resurrection day, having been washed and made white in the atoning
blood of the Saviour, may not find that correspondence witness
against us! There was in it no harm, but an absence of seriousness.
Which of us would like our letters buried with our friend if they
contain no healing balm – nothing to point to the Cross!'

Interesting that this incident in her youthful life should so many
years later have seemed so important that it should be remembered
in this way.

There is no mention in Lydia's Memoir, as published, of her move
to England, or of her time there. Her granddaughter, in editing this
for *Chambers' Journal,* wrote: 'On leaving Edinburgh, Miss Fraser
went to Surrey. There she spent two or three years with relatives who
owned a property in that county, and in whose beautiful home she
enjoyed much happiness and many social advantages'. She goes on to
say that Lydia's father then died; but she may have miscalculated her
dates because Lydia's Memoir shows that she must have moved to
England in the early Spring of 1829, after her father's death in June
1828.[9] In an unpublished essay written many years later, Hugh

9 The Memoir mentions the death of Mr Ballantyne's wife (mid-February
1829) 'about a year and a half after I arrived in Edinburgh'.

Miller's half-brother's son (who in fact had scant knowledge of family details) referred to some kind friends, 'the Dobsons', coming to the aid of the family, and to the children 'being placed in charitable institutions of the highest class'. This mention of 'Dobson' was the clue to discovering that Lydia had in fact gone to Egham in Surrey.

Thomas Mackenzie, Mrs Fraser's uncle who had left her £2000 in his Will, had a sister, Eliza, who had married a Robert Logan (possibly another planter from Jamaica). In 1815 Robert bought the substantial house, Egham Lodge (now demolished), overlooking Windsor Great Park. His eldest daughter and heir, Isabella, had married a Joseph Dobinson, a solicitor and Egham magistrate with an office in London. Eliza Logan was still alive (she died in 1846) and her nephew, Dr Thomas Mackenzie, also lived in Egham, so there would have been close knowledge there of Elizabeth Fraser's affairs, particularly of the business troubles of her husband, and of his death. This may have led to an offer to look after Lydia and her young brother, Thomas, while their mother coped with her immediate problems in Inverness. The charitable institution was Christ's Hospital School, to which Thomas, then aged seven, was admitted on 3 April 1829, sponsored by Joseph Dobinson.

The Dobinsons had four children born in 1820, 1824, 1827 and February 1829, while Dr Thomas Mackenzie had a daughter four years younger than Lydia and two other children born after 1821. Lydia may have helped to look after all these children, may indeed have given piano and other lessons to some of them. There can be no doubt that she was happy there. She called her first-born daughter Elizabeth Logan, in gratitude to the aunt who had been so kind to her. In her one published novel she placed her heroine in an idyllic home in England inherited from her baronet father, the description of which bears many resemblances to two large houses still standing, Egham Park, and an Elizabethan manor house, Great Fosters, in both of which she may well have been a guest. And there would certainly have been the 'social advantages' to which her grand-daughter referred.

This, as nearly as can be reconstructed from presently available evidence, is a picture of the accomplished young lady of eighteen, well educated, growing in sophistication as a result of her time in Edinburgh and Surrey, who joined her mother in Cromarty probably some time in 1830, and with whom Hugh Miller fell in love, and she with him.

# THREE

# Shining in Cromarty

'Accomplished' was a word which both amused and irritated Jane Austen by its universal application to young women however slight their abilities. But there can be no doubt that in 1830 Lydia was an accomplished young woman. Indeed, to judge by Hugh Miller's observations, there was perhaps something of the Austen heroine in her: the wit of an Elizabeth Bennet, a generous injection of Marianne Dashwood's impulsive temperament, the curiosity and social aware-ness of Emma Woodhouse, a good helping of the morality of Fanny Price, the credulous naivety of Catherine Moreland. As can be seen in her portrait painted a few years later, she was also pretty. It shows dark hair arranged in the style of the period with a knot on the back of her head and corkscrew ringlets either side of her oval face, luminous and pale complexion, eyes almond-shaped, dark and slightly hooded, a strong nose over a firm expressive mouth.

This 'accomplished' and pretty young girl now had to adapt to living in a very small and fairly remote Scottish town under the close supervision of a mother who was 'a lady of strong will and an unusual force of character'. It was a transition which she apparently made with ease, and it was her intellect as much as her prettiness which drew her into the company of Hugh Miller, who was to be so influential in developing her abilities to greater heights.

Mrs Fraser had probably chosen Cromarty to retreat to after her husband's death because of the presence there of two distant Cuthbert relatives, Mrs Flora Ross Taylor and Mrs Smith. It is clear that she fitted comfortably into that small community, of which she wrote warmly to her daughter in Surrey. In addition to the fisherfolk and other manual workers on whose labours its economy depended, there was a developing 'middle class' society of better educated people who, as noted by Hugh Miller in his story of William Forsyth already mentioned in Chapter One, came to form 'a circle of gentility' augmented by a number of ladies of 'lower pretensions' and 'a few retired half-pay ensigns and lieutenants', whose chief interest, perhaps, was in the exchange of hospitality in each other's houses. And, as in Inverness, little regard was given to the relative wealth of their neighbours, so that those like Mrs Fraser, with small incomes, would be as welcome as any in their parlours, while a man like Hugh Miller, with almost no money at all, would find himself in demand for the sake of his contribution to philosophical and literary discussions.

Mrs Fraser may have begun to take in a few pupils needing coaching before her daughter joined her, and Lydia herself soon set up a small school for girls, partly no doubt to be able to contribute something to her mother's modest income. She enjoyed teaching, however, and clearly liked living there, even before she fell in love with Hugh Miller. Her Memoir contains some vivid descriptions of its society and the way of life.

There was the retired Royal Marine Captain, Alexander Mackenzie of the Scatwell family, and his wife, who 'although but the daughter of a man who made his own fortune, had the finest manners [Lydia] ever saw . . . . Of a tall and commanding figure, reserved, and dignified conversation, she had the art – said to be impossible to those to whom it is not hereditary – of keeping people in their place by a look or by the gentlest word. Yet she was essentially most kind, and when a friend a very true one'. She and the Captain kept the only carriage in Cromarty.[10]

The Cromarty estate had no resident laird at that time, being heavily burdened with debt, so Cromarty House was let to a Mrs Colonel Graham of the Grahams of Drynie (in the Black Isle parish now called Knockbain). When she died, her son, Captain Graham of the Hanoverian Service, bought one of the largest houses in the

10  Mrs Mackenzie was the daughter of William Forsyth, 1722–1800, a prominent and successful merchant and farmer, and local benefactor, of whom Hugh Miller wrote in *Tales and Sketches* as already mentioned.

town, while Cromarty House was let to a succession of tenants none of whom stayed long. Several members of his family, 'all amiable, kind and good, always added to the charms' of this small society. There were 'two delightful old ladies – aunts of Sir Henry Barkley – thoroughly of the old school, who possessed a liberal income and spent it most generously. Their house [on the Braehead] was like a dispensary – not of medicine. Their table groaned with good things; and in those days it was no easy matter to rise from the table of old-school folks without something very like physical suffering'.

Robert Ross, later a banker who gave Hugh Miller his first proper job from which his subsequent remarkable career developed, was another prominent member of the social circle. 'Then a shrewd man of business [he had a pork-curing company] he had served in the navy, was particularly partial to the service, and had stored his mind in the most extraordinary way with the history of every naval engagement that ever took place in the annals of our country.' He knew the name of every ship and its commander 'and when he got upon that subject especially he was truly entertaining'. His daughters, Harriet, Isobella and Mary, became in their turns pupils of Lydia, as did their cousins, the Joyner children who lived next to the East Churchyard.

Mrs Allardyce, who came to Cromarty in 1834, became another friend. She was descended from George Urquhart of Greenhill (now known as Rosefarm and owned by one of Lydia's great-great-grand-daughters) and 'had a peculiar elegance of mind derived from long familiarity with the poets and writers, especially of the reign of Queen Anne'. One of her daughters, Catherine, who was a devoted admirer of Hugh Miller, had a strong interest in natural science and 'kept aquariums before these things were common, and educated herself without being indebted to any schoolmasters'. Another, Eliza, married Thomas Middleton of Davidston whose grandson, Thomas, married Lydia's granddaughter, Lydia Davidson.

Delightful distractions were provided by three warships at anchor in the Bay, of which 'the officers were always hospitably entertained by the inhabitants'. There were dancing parties, picnics and break-fasts to enjoy and the officers were great favourites ashore, including one Benjamin Fox, 'a fine young midshipman who had already won several medals of the Humane Society, and who was afterwards shot at the first siege of Canton'. A special friend of Lydia's – at least to begin with – was a young naval surgeon, William Cox, who told her that he had a great respect for Hugh Miller and spoke of him as 'a very remarkable man'. Cox confided in her that his captain, 'for whom by the way, he had a profound contempt', had warned him on the voyage north that 'he was coming among barbarians'. The surgeon had retorted coolly that he would find 'fully as much of every requisite for good society as he brought with him'.

Like all Cromarty society Lydia fell under the spell of the minister, the Reverend Alexander Stewart,[11] the power of whose sermons was such that she believed

> they would have served to mould the thought and opinions of men of the first capacities, if such had been his hearers, and of so great simplicity that no Sunday-school child or poor fisherman could come away without having some divine thought or image impressed on his memory for life. People looked forward from Sunday to Sunday for these sermons, and they formed the topics of conversations with high and low, even in casual forenoon visitings.

Indeed Peter Bayne wrote that Mrs Fraser had come to Cromarty because she wished 'to sit at the feet' of this man, which, given her own strongly evangelical upbringing and background, may have been true.

The elder of the two unmarried Smith girls – daughters of a former minister – was a particularly devoted admirer of Mr Stewart 'of whose sermons she took copious notes'. She also 'loved the deep things of Calvinism and enjoyed an argument (the more metaphysical the better)'. Lydia perhaps found her something of a trial, because

11 Alexander Stewart (1794–1847) was also Free Church Minister in Cromarty after the Disruption in 1843 until his death before he could take up the similar post at St George's in Edinburgh to which he had been appointed as successor to Dr Candlish.

she wished to engage me in deep discussion, which I, on the
other hand, sought to avoid. I liked a *raid* into the metaphysical
territory, but did not care to abide there . . . The younger, who
was of my own age, overflowed with what, for want of a better
word, I must call *human nature*. She had warm, sunny affections,
genuine humour, and an uncommon talent for mimicry which
hurt no-one . . . She would sit up all night with a sick child if it
belonged to the most miserable creature in the town. She was
my most beloved companion. How the woods used to echo with
our laughter on those long sunny afternoons! Happy days!
which come in a lifetime but once.

All these people became part of Lydia's new life, but as they were
also friends and admirers of Hugh Miller it is strange that she did not
meet him sooner, particularly as they lived on the same street only a
few doors apart. Her granddaughter says in *Chambers' Journal* that
Lydia had been told about this stonemason, who had published a
volume of poems, in a letter from her mother while she was still in
England. She knew that all her new acquaintances were proud of
Cromarty's stonemason poet, and yet she seems to have made no
effort to be introduced. Perhaps the age difference was too great, and
anyway she was busy with her school and flirting mildly with naval
officers. She herself put it down to the fact that their 'spheres lay quite
apart. I'm afraid I loved as much gaiety as I could get, while he lived
in his old contemplative, philosophical ideal'. Whatever the reason,
she did become interested in him after she had seen him, unobserved,
in June 1831 when she and her mother were visiting a nearby school
to watch the teaching method used there. Hugh came in shortly after
on the same errand (and published an article on his observations in
the *Inverness Courier*) and her mother told her who he was. Lydia was
'greatly struck by the thoughtful look of his countenance . . . He
seemed to listen attentively and to be lost in deeply abstracted
thought'.

Later that summer Lydia joined some friends who were talking to
him as he stood beside a sundial he had made. Hugh, in his 'letter
book' (much of which was later incorporated in *My Schools and*

*Schoolmasters*), recorded that he did no more than glance at Lydia on this occasion, but enough to notice that she was young and pretty 'and very much flurried, and that she deemed neither me nor my dial worth looking at. But though for the moment I ceased to be indifferent, I was not at all piqued. I perused her features for half a second and there saw the plumage of a fine bird or the petals of a beautiful flower and felt no way surprised that such a bright looking creature should find nothing to interest her in a moss-covered stool or a poor ungainly mechanic'. In *My Schools and Schoolmasters* he noted that 'though in her nineteenth year at the time, her light and somewhat petite figure, and the waxen clearness of her complexion which resembled rather that of a fair child than of a grown woman, made her look from three to four years younger'. Overhearing her exchanges with her friends, he thought she was 'light-hearted and amiable, but somewhat foolish and affected, and her friends who are much attached to her, love her less as an interesting woman than as an agreeable and promising child'.

Lydia was then, perhaps, although already a (very young) school-teacher, showing 'the flippancy of girlhood', to quote the felicitous phrase used by Hugh's distant and much admired cousin, Henry Mackenzie, in his novel *The Man of Feeling*, first published in 1771. Hugh had thought that on that occasion Lydia had not 'favoured me with a single glance', but he was wrong. She had deliberately chosen this opportunity to have a closer look at the man who had left such an impression on her at the school, and no doubt this was why she appeared 'flurried'. She for her part may have thought that he had hardly noticed her, and she may have been looking thereafter for ways of getting noticed.

That may have been her intention when a few weeks later Hugh met her while 'sauntering on a still and lovely evening through a solitary part of my favourite wood, my eyes fixed to the ground, my thoughts on the future'. Hearing a slight 'rustling through the leaves', he looked up to see Lydia (whom he now knew by sight) passing within a few yards of him reading a book, which he later discovered to have been 'an elaborate essay on Causation'. 'Had not my mind', he wrote, 'been preoccupied by the opinion of her I had so hastily formed, I would have finished the picture of beauty which opened to me as I raised my eyes, and which her presence so heightened – for a pleasant scene could not be furnished with a more appropriate figure by imagining of her as the Muse of the place and as elegant and accomplished in mind, and as lovely in form and feature.' No sign of recognition passed between them, but 'her face and figure in the accompanying landscape haunted me for several days after'.

Hugh had already made up his mind that he could not afford to fall in love. He believed himself 'to be naturally of a cool temperament' and that no woman of taste could ever be attracted to such an 'ugly and awkward' fellow. Nevertheless, he could not avoid some feeling of romantic love, and in his solitary walks he fancied himself with 'a female companion by my side, with whom I exchanged many a thought and gave expression to many a feeling', a 'day-dream lady' he called his 'bachelor wife'.

It was not long after this encounter that, meeting Lydia at a tea-party at her mother's where the only other guest was the naval surgeon, William Cox, Hugh's 'dream lady' began to materialise. Lydia, he was surprised to find, was 'highly accomplished and no fool, she drew finely, sang beautifully and possessed at least the endowments of a just taste in poetry and belles lettres'. He was disturbed, however, to notice that she was 'too desirous of being admired' and seemed to respond rather flirtatiously to Cox, whom he knew to be dissipated, with 'a kind of Don Juan smartness about him'. He wished he were in a position to warn her off fixing her 'affections on someone who gets drunk and is a rake'. Perhaps this was not conscious jealousy at this early stage in their acquaintance-ship, but his interest in Lydia had been sufficiently aroused to make him want to protect her from foolish fancies.

# FOUR

# Love's Awakening

Sometimes deep love between a man and a woman is recognised by both in a blinding flash on first meeting. More often, although both may have been aware from that first meeting of more than just a passing interest in each other, it is only after a period of what on the surface seems no more than enjoyable friendship and mutual respect that love is discovered. This was the case between Lydia and Hugh, and their circumstances were such that even when they did acknowledge to each other that they were in love, they had to wait several years before they could marry.

Lydia was at first troubled by the proprieties, for nothing in her experiences in the south of England had prepared her for the easy relationship which seemed to exist between her friends in Cromarty and someone who, whatever his apparent intellectual qualities, was only a poor artisan. She was content at first to meet Hugh in groups at tea-parties and on excursions into the countryside with her friends. There was a particularly significant evening in May 1833 when Lydia was walking with the Smith girl who so 'enjoyed metaphysical arguments'. They fell in with Hugh and had what Hugh later described as 'a long and very amusing conversation'. Lydia now began to look for opportunities to be alone with Hugh, after being assured by her mother's landlord, a magistrate and elder of the kirk, whom she consulted, that 'there was not a lady of the place who might not converse, without remark, as often and as long as she pleased' with him. She took to visiting him frequently in the church-yard where he would be engraving tombstones and monuments.

In her Memoir Lydia paints a vivid picture of Hugh as he then appeared to her (although this, of course, was a picture painted in retrospect very much later):

Hugh was essentially an aristocrat of the aristocracy of genius. He was born so; he could not help himself. He lived by himself among the great men of the past. Pope, Addison, Swift, Goldsmith, Burns were his companions, his real friends. He knew their histories intimately, and conversed with them perpetually in their works. Working, walking, visiting, he was seldom without some volume in his pocket. When dining out or at an evening party he was usually silent if the conversation were of a gossiping or personal description; but when an opportunity occurred for him to lead the conversation in his own way he never failed to embrace it, and the book in his pocket was often brought out to illustrate his ideas. His reading was remarkably pure and distinct, little tainted with any provincial accent . . . He had the faculty in a very singular degree of bringing the people to whom he spoke *up* for the time to his own level. His language, like his writing, was so simple and forcible that it was not possible to be stolid or impassive while listening to it.

Hugh's impressions of Lydia at that time were recorded more immediately than hers of him. He wrote that he had already decided, during that evening walk, not only that 'the greater half of the collective intellect of [Cromarty] is vested in the ladies', but that Lydia was 'by far the most intellectual of her companions'. And he began studying her character closely. At first it was her anxiety to please and her credulity which he noticed. Even her pupils, who adored her, were aware of her credulity. One of them, perhaps Harriet Ross, told Hugh: 'I never saw anyone like Miss Fraser. She believes everything we tell her'. Later, after being the only guest at tea at Mrs Fraser's 'with no one to divert her attention but myself', he

> perceived that her mind, though only recently awakened, was of no common order. She had begun to look into the nature of things, to analyse and to distinguish, to resolve causes into their effects, and to trace effects to their causes, and though there was much that was juvenile in her way of thinking and an apparent lack of skill in her style of argument, I saw that she was young, not weak, and only unpractised in thought, not incapable of it.

It was not long before they were able without inhibition to argue over philosophical issues such as the difficult Bible doctrine of Predestination. Lydia put forward 'a few simple *a priori* arguments that led her to conclude – infer at least – that since God is just, man must be free'. This was a subject of particular interest to Hugh, who was inclined to believe in predestination, and in arguing the matter with her he became quite intimate in his choice of examples. 'You were destined to be a very pretty girl', he said (according to his later recollection) 'and I to be an ugly red-haired fellow of five-feet eleven, but what choice did we have in that? . . . Only think of the subject and you will find St Paul quite in the right.' He further recollected that 'Miss F reddened to her very eyes and said nothing', apparently 'deeming my argument complimentary, although of compliment I had never thought'. Looking deeper into her character he found

some of those paradoxical discrepancies which render human nature a problem of such difficult solution. I perceived, or at least I thought I did, that she was in no slight degree self-willed, and yet not at all self-confident, and that she was formed to abide by her resolution whoever might disapprove of it or oppose it. And yet her love of approbation was so strong that she scarcely did or said anything without premising what others would think of it.

I deemed her to be one of those who sometimes fail of pleasing through an over-anxiety to please, and who when they act, come, as it were, out of themselves, that they may be at once the actors and spectators of the thing performed! Hence – and from her want of confidence in herself – from something in her manner which at times approached to affectation, and yet so much was she the reverse of being thoroughly affected that she was in general too open and too natural.

There was nothing in Hugh's own background which qualified him to be a judge of the psychology and personality of adolescent girls. Apart from being brought up in the company of two younger sisters, who both died when he was only thirteen, Hugh had had no experience, so far as is known, of companionship with girls of his own age. He was like most men of that era, assuming unto themselves a 'wise' and often pompously expressed judgment of the 'weaker sex' and the right to shape their lives. Nevertheless, he may have been shrewd in finding that Lydia's character was 'not yet fully formed and her mind immature and undeveloped'; in seeing that, as one who possessed a 'very unusual portion of cleverness', she was struggling to find a way of showing this without merely imitating the arguments she had heard and absorbed during her education in Edinburgh and experiences in Egham. Hugh may not have been fully aware at that stage of the background to Lydia's time in Surrey. But there she had been the 'poor relation' and, however kindly treated, she would have wanted acceptance of and an audience for her not inconsiderable talents. Even more would she have wanted to make a good impression in Cromarty society, and to extract as much enjoyment out of her life there as possible. She was not arrogant, vain or self-seeking, more the typical adolescent, eager for experience, unsure of her powers and touchingly naïve.

All this Hugh seems to have understood. But he saw further. He believed that 'the secret of her being so very accomplished' rested on 'the cleverness which enabled her to imitate well', that her whole youth had 'been one of acquirement', and that

> now that her higher faculties were gaining strength, she must necessarily quit the lower ground of mere accomplishment. Instead of imitating indiscriminately, she will find pleasure in only the exercises of superior minds and strive to obtain originality; and thus grown exclusively ambitious to excel in what perhaps she will not find one in a thousand able to appreciate, she will value the approbation of the superior few, and become indifferent to that of the mediocre many ... The cast of her mind is decidedly active. All her pleasures must be of a positive, not a negative kind, and she cannot indulge in indolence without becoming unhappy.

He was sure that her intellectual faculties were of the first order and that her reasoning mind was 'alike powerful and acute, nice in making distinctions, peculiarly happy in analysis and quick in illustration ... [although] ... not sufficiently careful of its first principles'. He considered her powers of observation of character to be marked (despite her apparent failure to see through young Cox), and active, with the ability to communicate the results of her observations as would a 'philosopher who analyses and separates into parts. She marks out the various traits, one by one, and resolves them into their first principles'.

*   *   *

It is not surprising that Hugh should have fallen in love with this young lady in whom he saw such a collection of contradictions: accomplished and well educated yet naive and lacking in self-confidence; flirtatious and eager to please yet often obstinate in her opinions and behaviour; sometimes affected and foolish yet gifted with a formidable mind; half child, half woman, and very pretty. Lydia's mother, however, was shrewd enough to realise that Hugh was falling in love with her daughter (and that Lydia too, although not yet aware of it, was probably also falling in love with him). She did not want her daughter to marry a man with no apparent financial prospects. So she forbade Lydia to see Hugh alone. This stunned Lydia for

Hugh was a friend of a higher order than I had ever even conceived, and under his guidance my mind, such as it was, began sensibly to develop itself. I felt like a poor little parasite which has succeeded in laying hold of some stately tree, and which a powerful blast has laid prostrate in the dust. I wept much, which confirmed my mother's suspicions. She feared I meant to content myself with the station of a mason's wife. She painted to me the narrow space, the rude meal, the sweat-and-dust covered mechanic returning to his poor home . . . [but] . . . I had not yet made up my mind to be Hugh's wife under any circumstances. The faintest conception of myself in such sur-roundings as these had never crossed me . . . My poor mother! She could not quite forget or smother traditions of family pride. Foolish thought, perhaps; but at any rate, from natural affection, she must have suffered much as she pictured for me a lot of hardship and poverty, with personal toil for which I was not constitutionally fitted.

But she was an obstinate girl who was not prepared to have her mother control her life, and she contrived to meet Hugh for evening walks on the wooded slopes of the Sutor, the hill behind Cromarty. Here, as Hugh, unaware then of Mrs Fraser's interdict, later recorded, they would 'witness together, from amid the deeper solitudes of its bosky slopes, the sun sinking behind the distant Ben Wyvis. These were happy evenings; the hour we passed together always seemed exceedingly short'. Love, however, was a subject which never came up in these discussions – until, after many months of such platonic meetings, as Lydia later recalled,

> one evening we encountered each other by chance in a wooded path of the hill, above which slope a few cultivated fields skirted by forest. Hugh Miller persuaded me to accompany him to a point which commanded a fine view of the firth and surrounding country. We sat down to rest at the edge of a pine-wood, in a little glade fragrant with fallen cones and ankle deep with the spiky leaves of the firs. I sat on the stump of a felled tree. He threw himself on the ground two or three yards from my feet. The sun was just setting, and lighted up the pillared trunks around us with a deep copper-coloured glow. Hugh took out a volume of Goldsmith. When did he ever lack a companion of that description? He read in a low voice the story of Edwin and Angelina. It was then I first suspected that he had a secret which he had not revealed.

Mrs Fraser must have found out about these meetings and spoken directly to Hugh, who now realised that he had been meeting her against her mother's wish. But he was by now definitely in love, and later told Lydia that from that day he had cut a notch in a beam of his cottage for every day he had not met her. Then came that chance meeting on a sultry evening in the late summer of 1833, and everything changed.

\*     \*     \*

Lydia, like many a young girl of slender means, may have dreamed while in Surrey of falling in love with someone rich and noble who would install her in an English mansion or, better, in a Highland castle. But she had matured and was no ordinary girl. Such fanciful dreams had long gone, and now she chose a man she could respect as well as love, someone who could stimulate her intellect. She had fallen in love not only with the best that Cromarty had to offer but also with one of the kindest and manliest of men, who could give her what she most needed, emotional security. What she did not know then was that she had chosen someone who was to prove to be one of the most complicated, brilliant and driven characters in Scotland at that time.

Mrs Fraser, of course, was shocked when Lydia told her that she was now in love with Hugh and wanted to marry him. There must have been long, probably tearful, arguments. Her mother would have warned her that marriage with Hugh would not be easy from the financial or social point of view. But Lydia was determined and her mother knew that Hugh was no mere uneducated workman with whom her daughter could not possibly ever be happy. She knew him to be a kind and considerate man with deeply held Christian beliefs. So, provided marriage was recognised as something a long way off, they were permitted to be engaged.

Hugh himself perfectly understood Mrs Fraser's attitude, which indeed he shared. In a letter to her written in November 1833 he said that until recently he had regretted neither his poverty nor his labouring life. He was industrious, contented and independent. 'I carried my happiness about with me, and was independent of every external circumstance.' Now, however, he had discovered 'that my happiness does not centre so exclusively in myself'. He realised that for Lydia's sake he would like to rise 'a step or two higher in the scale of society', although he recognised that this would not be easy because his lack of a formal education and his ignorance in business matters barred him from most professions.

Meanwhile Hugh had been having his poetry and articles published in the *Inverness Courier* from time to time. He now formed a plan. He believed he could become an editor of a magazine or newspaper and thus earn between one and three hundred pounds a year. In order to prove himself capable of such a post he decided to try and publish a small book (which was *Scenes and Legends of the North of Scotland,* eventually published in 1835). If the book failed, he told Mrs Fraser, 'I shall just strive to forget the last two years of my life, and try whether I cannot bring a very dear friend to forget them too'.

It was then agreed that the engagement should stand for the next three years on the existing basis, after which, if Hugh could find no suitable occupation in Scotland, they would emigrate to America, Mrs Fraser promising to let them have three hundred pounds from the bequest of two thousand pounds left in trust for her children by Thomas Mackenzie. Hugh did not doubt his own ability to make a life in America through hard physical work, but he was not sure that it would suit Lydia. She, however, with the optimism of youth and love, was prepared to meet the challenge. In her Memoir she wrote:

It is curious to speculate on what Hugh's career might have been if this scheme had been carried out. He might have begun with felling trees, but certainly would not have ended there. What a vast field the New World would have opened up for his genius, with no superincumbent social weight pressing upon him! But such dreams he never had. He often told me that his beau-ideal of happiness had been a very small competency which his own labour might realise – a sort of hermit-life devoted to literature, broken in upon only by an evening or a day occasionally with a true friend. 'See,' he would smilingly say, 'what a good philosopher you have spoiled.' I do not think he relished the idea of going to America. His temperament was the least sanguine I ever knew. For me, I looked upon it with the buoyancy of ten fewer years and with a disposition naturally more hopeful; but he seemed to feel himself condemned to a life of perpetual labour, to fell trees and dig and plant, a sort of toil he did not care for. Then his amor patriae was deeply seated in his breast. He loved to feel himself every inch a Scotsman. It was from Scottish history he drew his earliest inspiration. The

scenery, the traditions, the very soil of his country were inex-
pressibly dear to him.

Hugh's efforts to get his book published were unsuccessful. His
only hope seemed to be a subscription list, which he at first refused
to contemplate. Lydia offered to give him forty pounds which she
had saved up: 'if it will pain you to fancy yourself indebted to me
make it a loan – I shall indeed receive my own with usury when it
shall have been of service to you'. Hugh was deeply touched:

> Not all that industry ever accumulated could impart to me so
> exquisite a feeling as your kind and generous offer. My heart
> thumps when I think of it, and yet during the greater part of last
> night, for I have not slept for two hours together, I could think
> of nothing else. Could I avail myself of it, however, I would but
> ill deserve the affection which has prompted it. Money is not to
> you the thing you describe it to be; – there is little fear of either
> of us contracting a passion for it for its own sake, but as the price
> of independence (and in your circumstances it is peculiarly
> such) you must learn to value it . . . God bless and reward you; –
> every new trait I discover in your character while it draws me
> closer to you shows me how ill I deserve you.

But he refused it, and eventually he agreed to publish by subscription,
quickly raising the necessary three hundred signatures guaranteeing
eight shillings each to cover the cost of publication. Still, however,
there was not enough for marriage.

Hugh at this time had to spend much of his time in Inverness, from
where he would write to Lydia almost daily. She had seen the
manuscript of the book and had commented on it. Hugh wrote:

> Your criticisms, my Lydia, came rather late, but when I receive
> my proof-sheets I shall bring them you that we may talk over
> them. You are a skilful grammarian, but in some points we shall
> differ, – you know *we* can differ and yet be very excellent friends.
> I might try long enough ere I could find a mistress so fitted to
> be useful to me; – so little of a blue-stocking and yet so knowing
> in composition.

Indeed it is clear that Hugh had many discussions with Lydia not only about his prose but also on many subjects of mutual interest. But without his presence in Cromarty she was finding life there dull, and had told him so. 'You have embodied very happily', he wrote to her from Inverness, 'in your description, the yawning tediousness of some of our Cromarty parties, and caught to the life the tone of the sort of flippancy which has to pass in them for wit. 'Tis a sad waste of time, my own dear Lydia, to be engaged in such' — a foretaste of Hugh's reluctance later in their married life to accept social invitations. In another of his letters from Inverness he wrote:

It has been said, my own Lydia, that a philosopher in petticoats is a loveless thing; when I converse with you in this fashion, it is in the full conviction that few females' minds have been cast in a more philosophical mould than yours; but surely there is little truth in the remark, for never yet was there woman more warmly or more tenderly beloved.

They had their disagreements, however, and in this letter he made reference to one which shows that they could not always see eye to eye when it came to details of doctrine in religion:

However diverse in our tastes, however different in our opinions, however dissimilar in our philosophy, let us at least *desire*, my own dearest Lydia, to be at one in our religion. Whatever befalls us in the future, — whether from the edge of some solitary forest of the west our prayers shall ascend for assistance and protection, or whether in some happy dwelling of our own land they shall rise in gratitude to Him the benefactor, would it not be well for us, my dearest, that they should rise together addressed to the same God through the same Mediator, and in quite the same way; that each should be employed in seconding the requests of the other, not in internally lodging a protest against them?

Hugh had recognised that Lydia's background, education and sex had given her an outlook necessarily different from his own. These differences were superficial as long as they were able to agree on that one matter of fundamental importance to them both, their Christian faith. That Lydia kept this letter and gave it to Hugh's biographer indicates that she too was aware of the importance of its contents to their future happiness. Their Christian faith was the bedrock of their lives together, and Lydia supported Hugh wholeheartedly in his later part in the Disruption in the Church of Scotland.

\*     \*     \*

By the winter of 1834, when it was beginning to look as though even with the publication of Hugh's book, then with the printers, the backwoods of America might become a reality for them, Hugh received an offer which transformed their prospects. Robert Ross, the pork-curer who had served in the navy, had recently been appointed first agent of the Commercial Bank in Cromarty. He offered Hugh the post of accountant. Hugh at first was reluctant to accept; but after a while he began to realise that 'no man was ever born an accountant; and that the practice and perseverance, which do so much for others, might do a little for me'. He saw the hand of God in the offer, that 'it was one of the more special Providences of my life; for why should I give it a humbler name!'. And he accepted. It was a momentous decision, taken not with any great pleasure, for he had no desire to settle into a sedentary occupation, but because it offered, as Lydia put it much later, 'the prospect of life in Scotland with the woman he loved'.

FIVE

# A Long Engagement

Hugh had first to go South to be trained for his new job as accountant in the Commercial Bank, sailing from Cromarty to Leith on
27 November 1834. He was already well known by reputation in
Edinburgh. Back in 1829 the elderly Principal of the University, the
Reverend George Husband Baird,[12] who had met him on a visit to
Inverness, had offered him sponsorship, asking him to compose a
letter explaining how he was able to write so well despite his lack of
formal education. Hugh preferred not to take up the offer of sponsorship, but he did later (in 1833) write him a long letter in the form of
an autobiography, which eventually became the first part of *My
Schools and Schoolmasters*. He was also known for his *Five Letters on
the Herring Industry* (Chapter One). On reaching Edinburgh, he was
invited to dine with Sir Thomas Dick Lauder,[13] with whom he had
already been in correspondence, at his home, Grange House; but,
because he had found he was being sent to Linlithgow for his
training, he could not accept the pressing invitation to stay and call
next day on the publisher, Adam Black (1784-1847, later twice Lord
Provost of Edinburgh and Liberal MP for the city).

　　Although Hugh wrote almost daily to Lydia in Cromarty, he had to
wait some time for news of her in a letter dated 9th December, which
told him of her attending, along with many other young and not so
young ladies, a series of scientific lectures and demonstrations in
which she had taken a close and intelligent interest.[14] She realised

12　George Husband Baird (1761–1840) was Minister at Dunkeld in 1787 and
then at New Greyfriars Church, Edinburgh, in 1792. He became Professor of
Oriental Languages at Edinburgh University and then Principal in 1793.
13　Thomas Dick Lauder, 1748–1848, seventh baronet of Fountainhall (inherited 1820), was a contributor to the *Annals of Philosophy* and in 1839 became
Secretary to the Board of Scottish Manufactures.
14　These were probably given by the Reverend Mr Dickinson, who had for

Hugh would want to know about them. For instance, the lecturer had

> exhibited the gas of your bicubanous shell which bye-the-bye he
> calls merely 'parrot' coal. The gas, he says, is carboretted hydro-
> gen, just what is used for lighting the streets, but it seemed
> much more impure than what he produced yesterday from
> common coal. Neither underwent any purifying process. The
> spectators, especially the magistrates were hugely delighted.
> Mr Inger told me I should have much honour by the discovery.
> I answered that I was but the tongue of the trump and resolved,
> however, that though I let fame fly past me, I should not let her
> fly over my head. I proposed the plan of supplying the gas-
> works of Inverness and thereby obtaining town funds but I am
> afraid my wisdom was not taken up.

Lydia, it is clear, was able to follow such scientific explanations and
even to indulge in public banter. Moreover, she was interested in
public works for the benefit of the community, an interest which she
seems to have retained into later life, as she showed, rather eccentri-
cally, in her final Will (Chapter Sixteen). However, she was less than
enthusiastic over the experiments with electricity. She turned out to
be extremely sensitive to electric shock. In a lecture on Galvanism
she had been invited to experience one, from which she had suffered
'head-ache ever since and a considerable degree of nervous irritability'. Worse followed in another when, no doubt not wanting to
appear too timid, she agreed to be subjected to a shock from a 'voltaic
pile' which induced

> a violent trembling from head to foot. The crowd faded from my
> sight and I became insensible to everything. Dr Macdonald
> called the affliction hysteria, and I suppose the effect was hys-
> terical. Although not subject to hysterics, I know by experience
> what they are. But the sensation was altogether peculiar and
> unnatural. Oh, the horrible unnaturalness of it. I am yet far from

---

some years been Minister at Wick and was advertising such lectures in the
local press.

perfectly restored. To procure sleep, I have been obliged to have resort for the first time in my life to laudanum.

Perhaps it was the laudanum rather than the electric shock which caused

> the wild fearful thoughts and images which start into being between sleeping and waking [which] haunt me through the day . . . [until] this morning when your letter was delivered to me, I was almost fixed in the belief that I was suffering under a temporary derangement. God alone knows where I would have been today without it. It turned in part the current of my ideas.

It is possible that Lydia was over-dramatising this incident, but it was perhaps an early sign that her 'nerves' could be a weak point in her health. Hugh's reaction to this letter shows that he may already have been aware of this:

> 'Twas no wonder, my own dearest girl, that I should have felt so unwilling to open your letter, and that I should have looked twice at the seal to convince myself that it was not a black one. You are unwell, my Lydia, and here am I whose part it should be to soothe and amuse you, separated from you by more than 200 miles . . . Your temperament, my Lydia, is a highly nervous one; your delicate tenement is o'er informed by spirit; 'tis a hard-working system, and the slightest addition to the moving power deranges the whole machine. But be under no apprehension for your mind. Would that I were beside you to tell you how strangely I have sometimes felt when in a state of nervous irritability. The night before I received your letter, for instance, I had a world of foolish fancies about you; and my sense of hearing was so painfully acute, that I was disturbed by the noise of the blood circulating in the larger arteries.

Lydia was now taking advantage of school holiday times to visit friends of her mother's, many of whom would have been interested to meet the daughter who was engaged to this now already well known Hugh Miller. Shortly before Christmas 1834, she spent a few days

with the Taylors in Nigg, over the water from Cromarty.[15] Mrs
Taylor had taken her across in the ferry, and Lydia told Hugh that
'nothing could be better for me than the quiet cheerfulness of a united
and happy family, – they have all been so agreeable too and so kindly
attentive, – and the result is that I have got quite well'. In fact so well
was Lydia now feeling that she told Hugh of a plan 'to keep myself
active and cheerful by writing for the Annuals'. Hugh approved of
this:

> I am much gratified by your literary scheme. I have long ago
> told you that you are not one of those who can be at once
> indolent and happy; and I am sure you must often have felt that
> the remark was a just one. Your mind is highly active, and must
> have employment; and I know no exercise most [sic] suited to
> it than the one you propose. We must mutually assist and
> encourage each other, my Lydia, and should you be unsuccessful
> at first in forcing your way to the publisher's shop, you must just
> remember that there are few writers who have not failed in their
> earlier efforts . . . Genius itself seems hardly more indispensable
> to the literary aspirant than that mixture of firmness and self-
> reliance which, undepressed by failure or disappointment, can
> pursue its persevering and onward course till at length it
> triumphs over fortune and circumstance . . . at present your
> mind resembles a musical instrument of great compass and
> power, but nearly all the semi-tones are wanting.

But he added a cautionary note:

15  James Taylor was sheriff-clerk of Cromarty. He had been born in Tain and
had married Flora Ross, who had inherited property in Nigg from her brother,
Colonel Walter Ross, and was a close friend of Lydia's mother. Their children
adopted the surname Ross Taylor, and their daughter, Esther, married Alick
Middleton of Rosefarm, son of Thomas Middleton and Eliza Allardyce. Their
eldest son, Walter, Hugh's contemporary, was Free Church minister in Thurso
1843–96, and elected Moderator of the Free Church in 1884. His brother John
was Lydia's age, and in his turn also became sheriff-clerk of Cromarty. He
married, as his second wife, Harriet Ross, daughter of Robert Ross and Lydia's
great friend.

But, my own dearest Lydia, for your own sake and mine you must remember that your mind and body are unequally matched; – that though the one is strong and active, the other is comparatively fragile and easily worn out, and that your exertions must be modified to suit the capabilities of the weaker of the two.

\*     \*     \*

In January 1835 Lydia stayed with the Reverend Alexander Flyter and his family in Alness.[16] His wife, Elizabeth, was the eldest daughter of the Reverend Dr Ronald Bayne[17] who had influenced many of the outstanding 'Disruption Worthies of the Highlands' such as Donald Sage of Resolis, Alexander Stewart of Cromarty, John Macdonald of Ferintosh and Flyter himself. He had been an intimate friend of Mrs Fraser's family and largely responsible for her strong evangelical faith. His sons and daughters and grand-children in turn became close friends of Mrs Fraser and Lydia, his grandson Peter being chosen by Lydia to be the biographer of her husband Hugh Miller. The Flyters had seven children born be-tween 1817 and 1828. Lydia, in a letter to Hugh, described Alexander as 'tall and erect, with a snow-white head, a thoughtful brow, and an expression of finely blended firmness and gentleness, [who] was a conspicuous figure wherever he went, a man greatly beloved'. She commented shrewdly on the family:

> I was received at Alness with great affection. The increase of wealth there has not blunted any of the finer emotions of the heart . . . The spirit of the Presbyterian minister as he was in the days when the success of the Gospel was all to him, is kept alive in Ross-shire in perhaps greater strength than perhaps in

16 Alexander Flyter, born 1782 the son of a builder, was educated at King's College, Aberdeen, became schoolmaster of Fearn in Easter Ross, was ordained in Rothesay and translated to Alness in 1820.
17 Ronald Bayne (?1755–1821) was educated at Marischal College, Abeerdeen and was successively minister of the Gaelic Chapel there, Elgin, the East Church in Inverness and Kiltarlity.

any other part of Scotland. The ministers of the contiguous
parishes for many miles around meet every month in the house
of each alternative to inquire into the state of their parishioners
and to implore the aid of the Holy Spirit. Thus they pass a
whole evening . . . In politics my friends are high Tories, yet so
conscious that Toryism sits but ill on the Presbyterian clergy
that nothing is so disagreeable to them as to accuse them of
Tory sentiments. Nothing perhaps except to utter sentiments
that are not so.

One of the guests was a Gaelic-speaking Highlander and Lydia was
duly charmed. 'I sang and played and he showed a fine taste for
music. I repeated some verses. He criticised them at once with a most
just conception. The conversation became general. He showed the
best sense and the soundest practical observation. His grasp was not
extensive but his ideas were all clear and well-defined and he had
evidently thought for himself.'

After supper, the conversation turned to the Ossian controversy,
on which Lydia knew Hugh to be sceptical. The poetry of Ossian
was claimed to have been 'found' and translated by James
Macpherson. Hugh and many others believed that it had in fact been
composed by him. Lydia, however, thought differently, and she
deliberately teased Hugh: 'What burning thoughts must have
passed through the brain of Ossian!' she wrote. 'That a people with
such genius, and with such a language, should be deemed incapable
of producing such a poet! That those who have felt but for a moment
the spirit of Northern poesy could doubt ever after that Ossian
sung! Yes, annihilate the remains of Highland feeling and language
and manners, and then tell us that the question is decided, but not
till then. I am so exasperated at you that I would fain give you a
pinch.'

Certainly the poems of Ossian illustrate the genius of the Highlander, particularly that of a member of Clan Macpherson. Hugh
teased back: 'Dear me, what a red-hot Highlander you are!' And he
wrote most movingly of someone who to him was a true Highlander,
his cousin George Munro of the Gruids, Sutherland (Chapter One),

in whose parents' home he had originally heard the arguments about Ossian, and with whose family he had recently been staying in Stirling:

> I would not fear to match him, as a specimen of what his country can produce, against your Alness Highlander or any Highlanders you ever saw . . . Never was there a man more zealous for the honour of his country: he finds more mind in her poets, and more meaning in her language, than in the language and the poets of every other put together. Ossian surpasses Homer, and nothing can be more absurd than to question the authenticity of his poems . . . He has all the characteristic courage of his countrymen, and all their hospitality and warmth of heart . . . I read to him the part of your letter in which you describe the Alness Highlander and the Ross-shire clergy. His remark on your style you will deem a neat one. 'There are,' said he, 'more Mrs Grants than one.'

Which was a compliment indeed, for Mrs Grant of Laggan was not only known to Lydia, she was greatly admired as a writer.

Hugh was back again in Cromarty by the end of January 1835. His book *Scenes and Legends* was published in April and congratulations poured in. He found it difficult, however, to settle to a sedentary life, the only compensation being that although there were two more years to go before, as agreed with Mrs Fraser, he and Lydia could marry, they could at least meet more freely than before. But later that year she was away again, staying with the Macdonalds. Dr John Macdonald, called in his biography 'The Apostle of the North', was one of the most influential and charismatic ministers in Scotland who had a particular vocation for evangelism which took him out of his own parish all over Scotland and even, later, to England and Ireland. Indeed, this habit of 'itinerating' had brought down on him a rebuke from the General Assembly of the Church of Scotland on 30 May 1818 'that the conduct of any minister of the Church who exercises his pastoral functions in a vagrant manner, preaching during his journeys from place to place in the open air in other parishes than his own, or officiating in any meeting for religious exercises without the special invitation of the minister within whose parish it shall be held, is disorderly and unbecoming the character of a minister of this Church'. Lydia told Hugh that 'in Society no companion could be more agreeable. He was always radiant without ever making an effort to shine. The light of his countenance was spontaneous – he was pleased and therefore he was pleasant'. He can be recognised in the novel she wrote later (Chapter Nine).

It was during this visit that Lydia had her portrait painted, and it was only a few years ago that it was traced to the home of one of her descendants. In a letter to Hugh she names the artist simply as Mr Urquhart,[18] and describes him piquantly:

> He is a curious mixture of genius and stupidity. His comprehension and fancy seem deficient, while his drawing and colouring seem decidedly fine. He recognised me the moment I opened the door, which I rather wondered at as he only saw me once, and that four years ago; but not only is his memory in this way remarkably strong, but I have been told that he thought me like some painting of his . . . which would presume his recollection of me. He is tedious to a degree, has an odd whining kind of hesitation; is a whole minute in seeking a word to express his meaning which when found is either good for nothing or absurd; and his stories are interminable in every direction. I shall give you a grand specimen of his manner relating to yourself. He hunted for you till he saw you, and was asked by one of the Miss McDs what he thought of you. "Why – he has a very – peculiar countenance – he is a man of the most *infuriated* expression (meaning enthusiastic) I ever saw!"

When Lydia and Hugh were separated, she missed him badly: 'My own Hugh, I am tired, tired of being away from you. Alas! you have

18  This must have been Grigor Urquhart, who was born in Inverness about 1797 and died some time after 1846. He spent about nine years in Rome from 1818, after which he returned to Inverness. His main claim to fame is the copy he made while in Rome of Raphael's *Transfiguration*, which is now in the collection of the National Galleries of Scotland. He seems to have been a peripatetic portrait painter of no great talent.

no idea of the frivolous bondage to which sex and fashion subject us. I do nothing all day, and hear nothing, yet I am obliged to take the time from sleep which I devote to you'. And she was sure enough of their mutual love to refer, teasingly, to a 'young Captain' she had met, whom she found in fact

much handsomer than I described him to you, but a thousand times more insipid. Why, when I look at him, do I always think of you? or why do his black, bright eyes, that would be fine had they meaning, always remind me of those gentle blue ones which I have so often seen melt with benevolence and a chastened tenderness? Why are mankind such slaves of appearances as to admire the casket and neglect the gem? It is degradation to the dignity of thought and sentiment to compare it with a mere beauty of form or colour. Good-bye.

In response to this Hugh at least showed that his understanding of young women was now more mature:

You are fretted, my own dear girl, by the bondage to frivolity, which sex and fashion impose upon you. No wonder you should, when one thinks of the sorts of laws by which you are bound. The blockheads are a preponderating majority in both sexes: but somehow in ours, the clever fellows contrive to take the lead and make the laws, whereas I suspect that in yours the more numerous party are tenacious of their privileges as such, and legislate both for themselves and the minority.

He had discovered that Lydia was a woman whom he could love with physical passion, but also a friend and companion whose mind he could respect, someone who was confident where he was shy, formally educated where he was untutored, almost as well read as he. She had for him what he was to call 'the delicacy of the myrtle' to his 'strength of the oak', an analogy probably taken from Samuel Johnson's *Verses written at the request of a gentleman to whom a lady has given a sprig of myrtle*. Hugh's personal copy of the Poetical Works of Samuel Johnson fell open at this page when handled nearly two hundred years after his birth by his great-great granddaughter. And no doubt it was this that inspired Lydia to use the pen-name Mrs Myrtle when writing her books for children.

Hugh's and Lydia's prospects may not have been financially brilliant, but in every other respect they were good. This obvious mutual understanding, going well beyond mere physical attraction, was the strength that enabled their marriage to survive so well the coming tribulations.

# SIX

# Marriage and Early Sadness

Lydia was married to Hugh on 7 January 1837, just before her 25th birthday, by the Reverend Alexander Stewart. She records nothing of this occasion in the Memoir which has survived. Hugh, in his *Schools and Schoolmasters,* says only that he 'received from the hand of Mr Ross [Robert Ross the 'shrewd man of business' (Chapter Three)] that of my young friend [Lydia] in her mother's house, and was united to her by my minister, Mr Stewart'. But something of the ceremony was recorded more than thirty years later by Robert Ross's daughter, Harriet, in her (unpublished) 'Recollections of Hugh Miller' (now published as an Appendix to this book). 'This was a great event', she wrote, 'in the eyes of Miss Fraser's pupils, who looked up to her and loved her.' She described the scene in Mrs Fraser's drawing room as her future husband, John Taylor, had to come to her help when as part of her duties she could not get Hugh's glove off. And she remembered with particular pleasure Lydia's kindness as the couple left for their honeymoon: 'When having bade adieu to all, and received the hearty expression of their good wishes, I standing well behind older people heard the bride say "Where is Harriet? I must not go without saying good-bye to her!", and when on going forward she kissed me affectionately, I was a happy girl indeed'.

Both Hugh and Lydia recorded only brief impressions of their two-day honeymoon, which was spent in Elgin as guests of Isaac Forsyth, an elderly widowed banker who had always taken an interest in Hugh and his writing, having without success tried to promote his book of poems. Lydia, in her Memoir, was laconic: 'We were somewhat bored by a little man, the editor of a newspaper, who was mad upon Germanism, and poured out sentimentalism by the hour.

He said he meant to go and visit the tomb of Goethe, and there die. Hugh despised that sort of thing intensely; but he was very good-natured with the little man'. Hugh, writing to his friend Sir Thomas Dick Lauder only some eight months later, does not mention this boring 'little man', but is enthusiastic about the visit to Elgin, particularly their visit to the Priory of Pluscarden, Ladyhill

> with its rock-like ruin and its extensive views; the hospital, with all its wards; the museum with its spars and its birds; the splendid institution,[19] so redolent of the showy benevolence of the present age; and the still more splendid cathedral, so redolent of the showy piety of a former time; but above all, it was the hermit-like priory, in its sweet half-Highland, half-Lowland glen with its trees, and its ivy and all its exquisite innumerable combinations of the simple and the elegant, that impressed me most strongly.

He was equally enthusiastic over his new wife:

> I found, too, that my companion, whose taste had been much more cultivated than mine, was quite as much delighted with it. You, who are yourself so happy in your domestic relations, will not be displeased to learn that, after having enjoyed for full five years all that a lover enjoys in courtship, I now possess all that renders a husband happy in a wife. I have now been rather more than eight months married, and am as much in love as ever.

He had shown his love for Lydia also by inscribing a poem of his own in a pocket Bible which he presented to her just before the wedding:

> Lydia, since ill by sordid gift
> Were love like mine express'd
> Take Heaven's best boon, this sacred Book,
> From him who loves thee best.

---

19  In describing the honeymoon in *Schools and Schoolmasters*, Hugh mentioned that this 'princely institution' bore the name of Lt General Anderson by whom it had been built 'for poor paupers like his mother, and poor children such as he himself had once been'.

Love strong as that I bear to thee
Were sure unaptly told
By dying flowers, or lifeless gems,
Or soul-ensnaring gold.
[...]
His words, my love, are gracious words,
And gracious thoughts express:
He cares e'en for each little bird
That wings the blue abyss.
Of coming wants and woes He thought,
Ere want or woe began;
And took to Him a human heart,
That He might feel for man.
 [...]
Then oh! my first, my only love,
The kindliest, dearest, best!
On Him may all our hopes repose, –
On Him our wishes rest.
His be the future's doubtful day,
Let joy or grief befall:
In life or death, in weal or woe,
Our God, our guide, our all.

As Hugh himself, when including this in *My Schools and Schoolmasters,* wrote, it was 'prose, I suspect, rather than poetry, for the mood in which they [the verses] were written was too earnest a one to be imaginative'; and one must admit that, even judging by the type of sentimentality expressed in those days, they are hardly laureate standard. But they provide real evidence of the romance in this marriage.

On their return to Cromarty Lydia immediately began to set up their first home together in Miller House, standing on Church Street between the cottage where Hugh was born and the Courthouse. This substantial house of six spacious rooms on three floors, with a basement, was built forty years before by Hugh's father (but never lived in by him), and is now owned by the National Trust for Scotland

and being made into a Hugh Miller museum. The basement has gone and there are fewer steps leading up to the front door, but apart from the addition of bathrooms and some cupboards it is much as it was when Hugh and Lydia moved in. 'Our plenishing was not very great', wrote Lydia in her Memoir, 'but we managed to furnish a parlour and bedroom and kitchen pretty well and one of the attics had shelves put up for books and fossils . . . [and] a table and chair were set there by the fire' at which Hugh could write and study in the very few hours he had free from bank work for, 'although he perfectly understood the banking system, he took longer to the summing up of his columns than an ordinary accountant would have done. Consequently his hours were very long, and at the time of a balance extending till near midnight'.

Between them, Hugh and Lydia began married life with almost no savings, and their income was slender. But, as was usual for any family above the level of manual worker, they had a servant. Hugh was paid sixty pounds a year, which Lydia supplemented by giving lessons to Harriet Ross and her sisters, and teaching fisher-lads in the evenings. Hugh also made about twenty-five pounds a year writing articles for a weekly magazine edited by Robert Chambers, *Border Tales* (some of which later appeared in *Tales and Sketches*, edited and prefaced by Lydia in 1863). Somewhat reluctantly Hugh used this extra income for clothes, a subject on which he and Lydia never managed to agree throughout their married life. Lydia would have liked her man to give his mind to the dignity of his position, but he could never bring himself to do so. As Lydia wrote many years later:

To the body of the better and more intelligent working-men he was deeply attached. It was his *order*, to which he clung with chivalrous tenacity, all the more that he had perhaps felt keenly in former times the mean contempt of others graduating up-wards from the position into which he had now risen. It was this failing leaning to virtue's side which laid him open to remark on carelessness in attire from outsiders. If he had a weakness, it was that he liked to the last to carry some trace of a working-man about him, not from personal vanity, but from attachment to his old associates and respect for their grade. He loved the robust dignity of labour. With a working-man he could never bear to assume the airs of a superior. Yet I believe he honestly sought not to disgrace his new position.

Hugh had bought 'a little light yawl furnished with mast and sail that rowed four oars' and enjoyed using it before going to work in the summer to explore the coast with a geologist's eye. Sometimes he took Lydia and Harriet Ross out in it on summer evenings. Harriet in her *Recollections* remembered being often with them and that Andrew Williamson, Hugh's stepfather, and a cousin were the crew, showing that by now Hugh had become reconciled to his mother's second marriage. Andrew, according to Harriet, was 'rather talkative and not without some cleverness, but was what my father called "a trifling body"; however he seemed most willing to serve his step-son, whom he treated with great respect'. In Harriet's memory:

> We only went out on fine evenings, and as we kept as close as was safe to the shore we saw the rays of the westering sun clothing each outstanding rock and pinnacle, and the trees in the hollows on the summit of the Sutor with a golden veil, while the opposite sides of these lay in deepest shadow – a poor description this of what was exquisite beauty which caused a hush in the soul.

In fact a vivid description of a scene which can still be seen today. Hugh himself wrote that it was the long Saturday afternoons that were his

> favourite seasons of exploration; and when the weather was fine my wife would often accompany me in these excursions; and we not unfrequently anchored our skiff in some rocky bay, or even over some fishing bank, and, provided with rods and lines, caught, ere our return, a basket of rock-cod or coal-fish for supper, that always seemed of finer flavour than the fish supplied us in the market. These were happy holidays.

Lydia, however, like other young brides, had much to learn in the way of housekeeping, and Harriet, who had become almost one of the family, described in her *Recollections* how he good humouredly put up with his wife's occasional failures to have a meal ready for him when he came home from the bank to find her still busy with her pupils. Lydia, for her part, as she recorded in her Memoir, was amused rather than offended by the attitude of his devoted 'slave', Angus MacKay, a mentally handicapped boy he had befriended before the marriage. This lad would watch for hours for his 'hero' at the ferry if Hugh had been away on bank business to see if there was anything for him to carry

> or to accompany 'Miller' as he called him, home in triumph. A carpet-bag of his was a trophy to Angus; to rub away at his shoes, if he could get them was his heart's delight. I used to propitiate him with halfpennies; but I think he never entered quite into an understanding of the conjugal relation or found any use or necessity for me. The functions appropriate for a partner in life were rather performed, to Angus's apprehension, by the servant, whom he promoted to the dignity of 'Miller's wife'. It was a great source of amusement to my mother-in-law and other friends to ask Angie when he left our house, 'What was Miller's wife doing?' when he would answer, 'Frying flukes,' – or 'Washing potatoes,' or some such employment. 'And what was Miller's lady doing?' 'Sitting in the parlour.' I don't know whether there was not the least grain of contempt insinuated, as if 'the lady' were a personage who could be done quite well without.

Much of such spare time as Hugh and Lydia had was spent with the Reverend Alexander Stewart, who was a frequent visitor to their hearth, and they were both deeply influenced by this remarkable preacher, with whom Hugh would also take long walks. Lydia described him as

> tall, and in the pulpit extremely dignified, animated without noise, his gestures rare but emphatic. The conscious dignity of

his position as ambassador for Christ overpowered every other feeling. Earnestness is not the word that embodies him: it is too poor ... All personalities (and he was very singular), all vanities, all littlenesses were not so much forgotten as absorbed ... he would sit an hour or two – three when in a mind to engage in interesting conversation; but he could not endure close places and bad smells, and never tried. His mission was preaching, and that he fulfilled nobly ... What an interesting companion! – sometimes indeed, amusing you with whims and eccentricities, but often pouring out a wealth of originality ... He was one of those bright spirits about whose brows there seems wreathed even in this life a garland of immortal amaranth.

There were other visitors who came specifically to see Hugh because of his scientific discoveries. The young Dr John Grant Malcolmson of Madras, an amateur geologist who had become interested in Cromarty after reading *Scenes and Legends*, would want to spend evenings discussing fossil finds with Hugh while Lydia was busy with her sewing; but she found these rather trying: 'I didn't see just how these dead bones were to live. I sat at my work listening, wishing often that there would be a change of topic; but the interest of the two gentlemen was unwearied, their discussions unflagging too'.

Dr Fleming[20] was different, however. Lydia found his views and conversations 'greatly more discursive than those of Dr Malcolmson. He did not shut himself up in learning, he gave out clear, wide views on scientific subjects of general interest to a tyro like me, but fed by the intimate hard-earned knowledge within him, all the dry bones of which he kept to himself'. And it became clear, after Hugh's death when Lydia undertook the editing of his posthumous works, that she had absorbed much during such evenings, and from Hugh himself in their discussions and his later writings.

20 The Reverend John Fleming (1785–1857) joined the Free Church in 1843. He had been appointed Professor of Natural Philosophy at Aberdeen in 1834, and became Professor of Natural Science at the Free Church College in Edinburgh in 1845. He had published works on mineralogy and zoology in 1822 and 1828.

Hugh's and Lydia's happiness was crowned on 23 November 1837 with the birth of a daughter, baptised Elizabeth Logan. For Hugh 'little Eliza' was 'a delight and wonder above all wonders', and within a few months he found that

> home became more emphatically such from the presence of the child, that in a few months had learned so well to know its mother, and in a few more to take its stand in the nurse's arms, at an upper window that commanded the street, and to recognise and make signs to its father as he approached the house . . . Its few little words, too, had a fascinating interest to our ears; – our own names, lisped in a language of its own, every time we approached; and the simple Scotch vocable 'Awa, awa,' which it knew how to employ in such plaintive tones as we retired.

It was a short-lived happiness, however. In the summer of 1838 Hugh became seriously ill with smallpox, during which he experienced hallucinations. He had to be kept apart from his beloved daughter while Lydia, who had to give up her small evening class for fisher-lads and other occupations, nursed him. Then Eliza became ill, and in the Spring of 1839 Lydia had 'a close nursing of several weeks'. Eliza appeared to be recovering, but it was only a short remission. She died on 25 August that year, after three days and nights during which

> her father was prostrate in the dust before God in an agony of tears. Whether he performed his daily bank duties, or any part of them, I do not remember; but such a personification of David the king at a like mournful time it is impossible to imagine. All the strong man was bowed down. He wept; he mourned; he fasted; he prayed. He entreated God for her life. Yet when she was taken away a calm and implicit submission to the Divine Will succeeded, although still his eyes were fountains of tears.

Perhaps because they had walked there so often when they were first falling in love, Hugh and Lydia chose to bury Eliza in the ruins of the old chapel of St Regulus rather than in the East Kirkyard, the only one of the family to be buried in that lovely site. The headstone so beautifully carved by Hugh himself may still be visited today.

Lydia wrote a touching poem of which the following extracts from the full nine verses show the extent of her own grief:

> Thou'rt 'awa, awa' from thy mother's side,
> And 'awa, awa' from thy father's knee;
> Thou'rt 'awa' from our blessing, our care, our caressing,
> But 'awa' from our hearts thou'lt never be . . .
> [. . .]
> And art thou 'awa' and 'awa' for ever, –
> That little face, – that tender frame, –
> That voice which first, in sweetest accent,
> Call'd me the mother's thrilling name?
> [. . .]
> And does my selfish heart then grudge thee,
> That angels are thy teachers now, –
> The glory from thy Saviour's presence
> Kindles the crown upon thy brow?
>
> Oh no! to me earth must be lonelier,
> Wanting thy voice, thy hand, thy love;
> Yet dost though dawn a star of promise,
> Mild beacon to the world above . . .

# SEVEN

# Hugh Becomes a Newspaper Editor

The death of 'little Eliza' was a defining moment in the lives of Hugh and Lydia. It also coincided with a crisis in the Church of Scotland in which Hugh became deeply involved. This became an important influence in their marriage and in the development of Lydia as a woman, as a wife in the context of her generation, and as a writer.

Hugh, although a keen churchman, had taken little interest in the details of this crisis since it had become a public issue ten years earlier. He knew that there were those who wanted to separate Church from State and he knew that the Established Church was not without its faults. But he felt that 'a State endowment for ecclesiastical purposes . . . . had supplied the parish, free of charge, with a series of popular and excellent ministers, whom otherwise the parishioners would have had to pay for themselves', including his friend the Reverend Alexander Stewart. In 1838, however, he had felt compelled to interfere publicly in a local church dispute in Cromarty.

The date chosen in July of that year for the official celebration of the Coronation in 1837 of Queen Victoria coincided with Thursday Fast Day, an occasion of solemn preparation for the annual Sacrament of the Sabbath Supper. A small group of 'liberals' in the Cromarty congregation wanted the Fast Day moved to the Friday so that the Coronation celebrations could be attended by the faithful. Hugh thought this reasonable and persuaded Mr Stewart to agree. But Stewart was overruled by his Session who 'declined to subordinate the religious services of the Kirk to the wassail and merriment sanctioned by the State'. All twenty-five 'liberals', despite this, went ahead with their 'wassailing'. The matter then became a public issue in which supporters of the 'liberals' tried to make it appear that Stewart and his Session were in opposition to both the people and the Queen.

Lydia had felt as strongly as Hugh about the matter and with Hugh's approval wrote herself to one of the papers to try to set the record straight, but her letter was not published. Hugh then took up the case with a letter of his own, defending Stewart from charges of disloyalty to his sovereign, which brought down the fury of the 'liberals' on his head. He got a mild reprimand from his bank superiors in Edinburgh, but at the same time an offer of a newspaper editorship, which he turned down. Although he did not then realise it, however, this was the moment when he set foot on the road to his new career and his part in the Disruption in the Church of Scotland.

Although it was only in 1829 that the movement which led to the Disruption became visible, it had its origins much earlier and was coming to life by the beginning of the century. By then the Church of Scotland, influenced by Calvin and reformed largely by John Knox and, later, Andrew Melville, had fallen into a state of decline and was ripe for further reformation. Two factions became apparent: the Evangelicals, those who sought a re-awakening of old Calvinist roots, and the Moderates, who were seen as 'the party of polite learning and manners and support for the status quo'. Both, however, were opposed to the Dissenters, who were determined to disestablish themselves from the Established Church of Scotland and, even more significantly, disendow the Presbyterian Church. The active campaign – called the Voluntary Controversy – was begun with a sermon in Glasgow in 1829 by a dissenting minister, the Reverend Andrew Marshall, who declared that religion was at its best when voluntary and unconnected with the state. Also it was not fair to give one Church privileges and endowments and force non-members to support it. In 1833, the Voluntaries decided not to pay their Church rates in Edinburgh, which caused serious financial problems for the Established Church. By 1834 the Evangelical party outnumbered the Moderates in the General Assembly of the Church of Scotland and claimed to be the only party able to preserve the Established Church and its basic principles.

The leading figure in the Evangelical party after 1831 was the

Reverend Dr Thomas Chalmers who believed passionately in an improved and revived parish system, and in the 1646 Westminster Confession of Faith, the dogma of the Established Church. However, the Evangelicals were not in favour of Church patronage, a practice begun with the formation of the parish system in the twelfth century that allowed the owner of the land to choose the parish clergyman. Most parishes in Scotland had their legal patrons, who might be the Crown, the gentry, the burghs or the universities. At the very beginning of the Reformation in 1560, patronage had been abolished and congregations given the right to elect their minister. Various Acts over the years, however, had modified this decision until finally the Patronage Act of 1712 gave a landowner the right to choose provided the senior male parishioners agreed to 'call' the appointee.

Under the Moderates, this 'call' had degenerated into a mere formality. The candidates put forward by the gentry were upheld in spite of occasional fierce opposition by the parishes. Patronage where the landowner intruded an unpopular minister was responsible for large numbers of Church members seceding and joining one of the newly formed secession churches. When the Evangelicals outnumbered the Moderates in 1834, the General Assembly passed three reforms. First was the Veto Act, a compromise in that it allowed the male heads of churchgoing families the right to veto the patron's choice. This was not a new law but a means of restoring the terms of the Patronage Act of 1712. Second was the Chapels Act which gave status to the new churches built in overcrowded areas or distant areas – there were forty of these congregations in the Highlands alone – as *quoad sacra* parish churches, in other words, churches with spiritual power over defined areas whose ministers and elders had full legal rights. The Assembly hoped that this act would not only encourage new church building but also persuade seceding congregations to return to the fold.

Thirdly, the Assembly inaugurated the Church Extension Committee to encourage a national campaign for building new *quoad sacra* churches. This Committee was under the inspired leadership of Dr Chalmers, whose vision of a new future for parish communities was built around his own experience as a parish minister at St John's

Church in Glasgow some years previously. Under his tireless zeal and inspiration, local and provincial branches of the Committee flourished. From sums upwards of a penny a week from the poor, money poured in from the parishes so that within seven years over two hundred and twenty new churches were built. Other Committees were formed to organise Education, Foreign Missions, Colonial Churches and the Mission to the Jews. More Evangelicals entered the ministry and patrons became more careful and conciliatory over their presentees. Parish churches began to imitate the ideals of Dr Chalmers. By 1838, when the Evangelicals celebrated the two hundredth anniversary of the signing of the National Covenant, it seemed as if the Church of Scotland was returning to its original high principles.

Not everyone, however, approved of the Evangelicals. The older landed gentry, the professional elite and the Moderates found themselves embarrassed by the display of zeal, the emotional charismatic preaching and the stern Calvinistic outlook frowning on the pleasures of life. The Voluntaries too were strongly opposed to the Church Extension scheme which they saw as a real threat to the aims of the Dissenters, disestablishment. Thus there developed a harsh struggle between the Church Extensionists and the Voluntaries with angry words written and debated at meetings and in the press. The Voluntaries managed to convince the Whig government that there was no need for new churches if the Dissenting congregations were taken into consideration. So, in 1835, the government appointed a Royal Commission to investigate the matter of church accommodation in Scotland and invited the Dissenters to give evidence.

In March 1838 the report of this Commission was published and the government announced that it did not see the need for new building and therefore would not provide endowments for any more Established churches. The Duke of Wellington, then leader of the Conservative opposition in the House of Lords, informed members of the Church Extension Committee himself: 'Gentlemen, you will get nothing; I am sorry for it; but so you will find it. You have two parties against you – the Radicals, with Lord Brougham at their head; and the Government, who are really as much opposed to you as the Radicals'.

This was an enormous blow to Dr Chalmers and his hardworking Church Extension Committee who felt betrayed by the state. But worse was to follow. The Veto Act had seemed to be working well, with compromises made both by the patrons and by the congregations. Out of one hundred and fifty appointments in five years only ten were vetoed. The main difficulty, which had probably not been foreseen, occurred when unwanted candidates appealed against the veto. The first of these appeals was made by Robert Young, who had been presented by his patron, the Earl of Kinnoull, to the parish of Auchterarder in 1834 and vetoed by two hundred and eight-six votes to two. Young appealed to the Ecclesiastical Court of the General Assembly, which upheld the veto. He then appealed to the Court of Session, which found for him on the ground that the Veto Act, a church law, had no existence in civil law.

Two further patronage confrontations in 1837 were also significant. The first was in the parish of Lethendy in the Presbytery of Dunkeld where a certain Thomas Clark had been appointed by the Crown, patron of the parish, but had been rejected by the congregation. Although the Crown then presented another, acceptable candidate, Clark too appealed to the Court of Session, with the same result. The second confrontation arose when the Earl of Fife offered the parish of Marnoch in the presbytery of Strathbogie to the unpopular assistant minister, John Edwards. The veto was unanimous bar one. Here too the patron accepted the decision and offered a satisfactory alternative candidate, but Edwards in his turn won a decision in his favour from the Court of Session.

A new party, known as the Non-intrusionists, now appeared on the scene. They were solidly against the 'intrusion' of patronised candidates into parishes against the will of the congregations. They comprised nearly all the Evangelicals and were led, unsurprisingly, by Thomas Chalmers, who had been so deeply hurt by Parliament's opposition to the endowment of Church Extension. Remembering the history of the Reformation, the Non-intrusionists insisted on the doctrine of two kingdoms, the one spiritual under the headship of

Christ and the other temporal under the Crown and Parliament. The Church could not in true conscience surrender the sovereignty of Christ in matters spiritual. This spiritual sovereignty included the ordination of ministers and ecclesiastical discipline.

The General Assembly of 1838 had been divided in its approach to the civil judgement in the case of Robert Young in the parish of Auchterarder, so the case was taken to the highest court in the land, the House of Lords, for a decision concerning the settlement of ministers. On May 4 1839, the Lords decided for Young and Kinnoull, and declared the Veto Act to be illegal. Lord Brougham, who five years previously had congratulated the General Assembly on their Veto Act, now declared that the opinion of the parishioners had always been a mere formality, 'comparable to the actions of the champion's horse at the coronation ceremony; the opinion of parishioners, whether expressed through a call or a veto, could have no effect on the patron's rights or the obligation of the Church to ordain a licensed presentee'.

It was Chalmers who, at the General Assembly in 1839, first raised the possibility of a disruption between the Church and the State if civil courts were allowed to overrule the Church courts in matters of ordination and ecclesiastical discipline. And it was in 1839 that Hugh, who had up to then been 'thoroughly an Establishment man', decided to join the debate. He 'saw with great anxiety decision after decision go against' the Church, and saw 'as one entanglement succeeded another, confusion becoming worse confounded'.

He and Lydia had already come under the personal influence of Dr Chalmers, whom Hugh had long looked up to as 'the man of largest mind which the Church of Scotland had ever produced'. On the last of his Church Extension visits in 1839, Dr Chalmers had paid a call on the Millers in Cromarty. They had then heard 'for the first time, that most impressive of modern orators address a public meeting, and had a curious illustration of the power which his deep mouth could communicate to passages little suited, one might suppose, to call forth the vehemency of his eloquence'. Hugh had spent a day with him visiting the Sutors by boat. Lydia too was impressed: 'Dr

Chalmers's visit was a short one, a forenoon call. Nevertheless it was the first time we had seen that great man in private, and we were struck, like everyone else, with the goodness, the large humanity, which only a near interview in private made one fully sensible of. His call, his address in the church, and the sail with Hugh round the entrance to the bay were altogether a charming bit of sunshine'.

Following a sleepless night caused by reading the speech of Lord Brougham, Hugh 'sat down to state my views to the people', in the form of a letter addressed to Lord Brougham. Coming about a month after the death of little Eliza, the composition of the letter may have helped to take his mind off the agony of his grief. Perhaps Lydia too was helped by being involved in its drafting. The result was a masterpiece of reasoned argument and flowing language. But the elegant prose – it took a week to complete – did not hide the indignation, pain and outrage that Hugh felt on behalf of his Church.

After paying due tribute to Lord Brougham as a reforming politician (who had once approved of the Veto Act) and describing himself as 'a plain working man . . . whose opinions . . . regarding the law of patronage are those entertained by the great bulk of my countrymen, and entitled on that account to some little respect', he asked the question 'Where is the place which patronage occupies in this Church of the people and of Christ?' His answer was simply that it held no place. And the final paragraph was not only an inspired piece of writing, but prophetic in the true sense of that word. It described with controlled emotion not only Hugh's beliefs with regard to the Church he loved, and Lydia's – which was to become evident in her novel published eight years later – but that of so many of their fellow countrymen:

> The Church has offended many of her noblest and wealthiest, it is said, and they are flying from her in crowds. Well, what matters it? – let the chaff fly! We care not though she shake off, in her wholesome exercise, some of the indolent humours which have hung about her so long. The vital principle will act with all the more vigour when they are gone. She may yet have to pour forth her life's blood through some incurable and deadly wound;

for do we not know that though the Church be eternal, churches are born and die? But the blow will be dealt in a different quarrel, and on other and lower ground, – not when her ministers, for the sake of the spiritual, lessen their hold of the secular, not when, convinced of the justice of the old quarrel, they take up their position on the well-trodden battlefield of her saints and her martyrs, – not when they stand side by side with her people, to contend for their common rights, in accordance with the dictates of their consciences, and agreeably to the law of their God. The reforming spirit is vigorous within her, and her hour is not yet come.

The repercussions were unexpected and of enormous significance for Hugh and Lydia.

Hugh had sent a copy of this letter to Robert Paul, head office manager of the Commercial Bank in Edinburgh and a good churchman. On a chance meeting with Dr Robert Candlish,[21] minister of St George's, Edinburgh, Robert Paul gave him the letter to read. Candlish, who had never heard of Hugh, was bowled over by what he read. 'I never can forget the rapture, – for it was nothing short of that, – into which the first pages threw me', he later wrote to Lydia. A few days later, Henry Dunlop[22] and Robert Paul decided to invite Hugh to become editor of the newspaper they and others were about to set up, *The Witness.*

Without revealing the reason, Robert Paul wrote to Hugh suggesting that he visit Edinburgh to meet some gentlemen who thought his talents could be used 'in some literario-Christian way'. Hugh was given leave by Robert Ross from his bank duties, and he and Lydia, travelling by sea from Cromarty, became the guests for a

21  Robert Smith Candlish (1806–1873) was minister at St George's from 1833 after being assistant minister at Bonhill, Dumbartonshire. He had taken a leading part against the authority of the civil courts in patronage cases and joined the Disruption in 1843.
22  This may have been Henry Dunlop (1799–1867), a Glasgow merchant who was Provost of Glasgow 1837–40 and President of the Glasgow Bible Society 1850–61.

few days of Robert Paul and his family. They were both surprised to find Hugh was 'lionised' in Edinburgh because of his letter to Lord Brougham. And it was not long before they were guests at a dinner party with several prominent churchmen and the true reason for the invitation to Edinburgh was made clear.

Hugh immediately realised the importance of what was proposed. Out of the sixty-three newspapers then published in Scotland, only eight supported the Non-intrusionists. The failure of the first to be set up specifically to advocate the cause might not lead to the failure of that cause, but it would be a 'sad discomfiture and sore disgrace' as Lydia put it later. Moreover, Hugh knew that the twice-a-week demands of a national newspaper, the editor of which 'writes in sand when the flood is coming in' as he put it, would take up all his time. He believed he would have to give up his beloved geology and feared he would never have time to make his mark on the literature of his age as he hoped to do.

Hugh hesitated long before accepting, but accept he did. Given the closeness of their love, it is unlikely that he would have done so against Lydia's wishes, had they been strongly expressed and well argued. But in fact she herself saw the offer as a great opportunity for him to fulfil his potential, and she may have argued him out of his own doubts. 'Perhaps', as she wrote so many years later in her Memoir,

> I did not see all the difficulties; my confidence in his powers was greater than his own; my appreciation of the position, from the inferior grade of mind, was less. I see it, now that the din of conflict and the dire results of the battle are before me, better than I did then. Whether this was the best or not I cannot say. If I had been more clear-sighted, I, too, might have shrunk back in dismay, and might not have used what influence I had in the onward direction . . .

She would also, no doubt, have had in mind that it would bring its financial rewards and so improve the family's standard of living. But she was probably being self- deprecating in continuing:

To dress better, to live in a better house, to have daintier fare – all these were things to him as if they were not. Indeed, the absence of that ordinary kind of ambition in him might be said to amount to a fault. I might want respectable tables and chairs, and take pleasure in painting and garnishing my house, and he might look upon all this as something to be expected in the feminine gender, and to be tolerated accordingly.

But at the time Lydia had no such doubts, and she now looked forward with eager anticipation to what seemed to her a just reward for Hugh's abilities. She did not then know that the halcyon days were over.

# EIGHT

# Edinburgh and the Disruption

After accepting the offer of editorship of *The Witness* Hugh remained in Cromarty for six more months, partly, no doubt, to give time for his successor at the bank to be found, but also because Lydia was pregnant. During this time, Hugh, as Lydia put it, took 'pleasure where he could – for that was rare – in sitting with fossil-shelves and book-shelves around him, and with a heap of literary confusion about, which was order to him, and which no hands might touch. And if I came in and sat on his knee and talked to him a little, that was his paradise'. When Lydia became ill after the birth of their second daughter, Harriet, on 25 November 1839, he had to make a doubtless difficult choice between staying longer with her and getting to Edinburgh in time to oversee the first edition of the paper due out in early January. But the paper had to come first and, after being guest of honour at a public dinner in Cromarty when he was presented with a silver tea service, he sailed for Edinburgh in late December to face a new challenge on his own.

*The Witness* had been set up with a capital of a thousand pounds to which many prominent Evangelicals had contributed. Hugh, who had accepted a salary of two hundred pounds a year which was doubled after three years, had insisted that it should be a proper newspaper with news coverage, not attached to any particular political party. It was to be above all a champion of the spiritual independence of the Church. Published twice a week, it kept Hugh working harder than he had ever done before, and it was not surprising that by the time Lydia was able to join him in the Spring of 1840 he was looking pale and ill, having only just recovered from a bout of 'flu.

Lydia and the baby were accompanied by a nursemaid and a

servant, and by the seventeen-year-old Harriet Ross (who had been ill during the winter and had been invited by Lydia to go with them to seek medical advice, in the event staying until the end of July). It was a stormy sea journey and they arrived only late on a Saturday evening at Granton. In her *Recollections* Harriet wrote:

> Mr Miller had been waiting for us since the morning, and must have been faint and weary though he did not show it but said he had been geologising, and so kept his mind and body occupied. Sea-sickness had so prostrated me that I hardly remember how we got up to town; but we were set down at the east end of Princes Street, in the midst of a crowd under the theatre which then stood there; and its glaring lights illuminated in weird fashion the faces of probably not the choicest class of citizens. But we did not stand long there but soon drove on by the Bridges to St Patrick's Square where Mr Miller lodged in the house of a young artist with whom his mother and the younger members of his family lived. It was a clever family struggling hard to earn a respectable livelihood, and sympathy with them had, I think, much to do with Mr Miller's choice of lodging.

This tenement flat was four stories up, where Hugh's accommodation was simply a bed-sitting room 'dingy with dust and littered with papers' as Lydia later told Peter Bayne. Indeed Lydia was not so generous as Harriet in her memories of this family, for in Bayne's *Life and Letters* this son 'took the style of an artist and sat painting in the principal drawing room' while another 'cultivated poetry' and 'the only daughter spent a large part of her time in the practice of singing, with a view to appearing before the public. She accompanied herself on the piano, and her shakes and bravuras, on which she industriously lingered, would not have a soothing effect on Hugh's nerves while engaged with his articles'. But then Lydia did have a hard time of it at first, so it is perhaps not surprising that her memories were bitter. Hugh had assumed that they would have been able to find more suitable accommodation for the first night, but the late arrival made this impossible so, as Harriet put it, they 'managed somehow till Monday when all were made more comfortable'.

This was hardly the joyful return to Edinburgh to which Lydia had been looking forward, and it is not clear how long they had to stay in temporary accommodation before moving into the house Hugh had already arranged to lease at No 5 Sylvan Place, 'the furthest up the lane on the south side of the Meadows'. This was a happy choice. It had relatively open country to the south and a small railed garden in front. Behind was a large grassy enclosure backing onto a market garden. A small whitewashed dairy surrounded by trees was at the far end of the lane. Harriet Ross recalled that 'from the windows in front we saw Arthur's Seat, and from the drawing-room windows an extent of the richly green meadows with fine trees here and there'. But, as Harriet recalled, 'the days which followed were fatiguing ones for Mrs Miller for the house ... must be furnished and she had to be out the livelong day making purchases', adding with delightful candour: 'Her husband was too busy to help her, and even if he had leisure would not have been well suited to the task'.

Lydia and Hugh had decided to sell their Cromarty possessions before Lydia left. Unfortunately the day of the sale had been so cold and wet that few people had turned up. Their household goods, valued at £150, had fetched a mere £40 which was all she now had to spend. Hugh refused to allow anything to be bought on credit, so she had to attend sales and look for bargains. Eventually in this way she was able to furnish most of the rooms except for the drawing-room, but according to Harriet Ross 'a few things were put into it and we found it a pleasant sitting-room. Books which we had brought from Cromarty, and many new ones which came to Mr Miller as the editor of a newspaper were piled up around the walls, and at the foot of the room which was not a small one, his desk was placed. There he wrote all the long day and far into the night except on Wednesday and Saturday afternoons when he took long walks into the country'. But Harriet remembered that one Wednesday he took them to Greyfriars churchyard to see the 'newly-made grave of Miss Fanny Allardyce', the daughter of the Mrs Allardyce already mentioned among the Cromarty society.

Life soon settled into a routine. In the evenings, Harriet recalled,

'Mrs Miller and I sat either working [ie sewing], reading, or writing, and took good care never to disturb Mr Miller. He never sat, but walked up and down, repeating his sentences until they were moulded to his liking; occasionally coming up to his wife and saying, "Do you think this is the best way to put it?" and when satisfied went to his desk and wrote . . . At meals that on which he was writing was the subject of conversation, for we were generally alone and often a book was laid on the table out of which something was read . . . [At night] although my room was not quite near the room in which Mr Miller wrote, I could often hear him speak loudly as if arguing with an opponent. I have known him write continuously for eleven hours, and I heard him tell his wife that after writing many hours a pain seized him in one particular spot in his head on which he laid his finger, and she said, "O Hugh, take care that you don't injure your brain".' This premonitory remark is where the surviving part of Harriet's *Recollections* ends.

Lydia helped Hugh when she could. As soon as she had made the house habitable she began 'to assist in the editorial department first with paste and scissors, then with pen, as contributor of reviews of books, earning thereby some £20 per annum, which went to the furnishing'. One morning Hugh returned in great spirits after breakfasting with Dr Chalmers: 'The great man had complimented him on one of *The Witness* critiques, and he had never felt so proud in his life as in saying it was by his wife'.

Meanwhile baby Harriet was flourishing. 'Ha-Ha', as she called herself, was 'an uncommonly lovely and attractive child', fair with azure-coloured eyes and golden curls which reached to her waist. Hugh once asked Harriet Ross if she thought her like her sister, Eliza. 'There was a family likeness, nothing more. Harriet was the prettier child, and she was spared to grow up a pretty and clever woman; but there was a wonderful depth of expression in the baby Liza's face'. Little Ha-Ha inherited qualities from both her parents. Peter Bayne quoted Lydia as saying she was

naturally refined, with great elegance of figure, she glanced about the house like a sunbeam, her childish voice bursting out in a continual ripple of prattle and song. Song more often than prattle – for she was one of those children richly gifted *as* children, with a certain genius blended with infantile graces which sometimes develops with the growth, sometimes falls away like the blossom of a too early spring. Such was Scott's pet Marjory. Little Ha-ha, however, had one gift which I have never met with in any other child. It was that of natural improvisation. Every little incident, every phase of feeling, was embodied in song and poetry, which would continue through a long summer's day. The music was always full of melody, the poetry a sort of measured blank verse, sometimes rhyming and sometimes not.

One of Hugh's admirers in Edinburgh, who also became a close friend of Lydia's, was Marion Wood, whose brother, the lawyer J G Wood, was one of those involved in the setting up of *The Witness*. Peter Bayne, in *Life and Letters*, quotes from *Recollections of a Lady by M W*:

> Hugh Miller dined at our house . . . I had the good fortune to sit next to him and we had a good deal of conversation . . . When his family came to Town it was with much pleasure I recognised in Mrs Miller a fellow class-mate. This led me frequently to her house and gave me the opportunity of meeting her husband. There could be no greater or more exciting pleasure than to converse with Hugh Miller.

One of her happiest memories was of a summer evening after a dinner-party with the Millers at Sylvan Place, when they all walked up Blackford Hill. The men, all boys at heart, decided to see who could throw the furthest stone. Hugh won easily, no doubt pleased at this exhibition of his physical strength. On another evening the conversation turned to ghosts:

> I have never heard such stories so told . . . he seemed to see the scenes he described, and compelled one to see them too. It was evident he had been nurtured in the belief of these superstitions, and that in early life they must have had complete sway over his

mind, – a sway that might be resumed in hours of weakness. Then, however, he disclaimed all belief in them; and in the conversation which preceded the stories, had made some forcible remarks on the frequent combination in the same person of scepticism and credulity, and on the difference between a real faith in revealed truth, and the ready belief in lying wonders, then beginning to be common.

In these first few years in Edinburgh, Hugh and Lydia were little better off financially than they had been in Cromarty. But, even though they had to watch their expenditure carefully, Hugh sent an allowance of five pounds a quarter to his mother and small sums to his aunts. Hugh's work for *The Witness* was the centre of family life, which developed its own routine. Supper together was their favourite meal. Breakfast was merely coffee and some bread. Hugh did, however, manage to maintain his interest in geology. After working at his desk for some hours, if there was nothing urgent to attend to he would 'saunter about the hills of Braid or Arthur-seat, explore for the thousandth time the Musselburgh shore or the Granton quarries'. But 'he never clearly admitted the canonical authority of the dinner hour' on such occasions, not necessarily being back in time to share the meal with his family, expecting it to be kept warm for him. It was often dark before he returned and it was not until about 10 pm that he became really hungry. Lydia would then provide him with his glass of porter or ale, and a snack of dried fish or preserved meat. This was their private time together as a couple when they could talk and debate freely. As Bayne put it, 'There can be no doubt that the extraordinary success of many of his articles, – the repeated case of their being the town-talk and country-talk of the day, – was due, in a considerable degree to his having beaten over the ground with Mrs Miller'.

Their social life had its problems. Bayne wrote: 'That section of Edinburgh Society, the literary men, which Miller would have found at heart most congenial, was closed to him by the religious animosities of the time'. But in the *Annals of the Disruption* it is stated that while the Literati upheld the Moderates, the lawyers and physicians supported the Free Church. George Thomson and his circle were Moderates, so Lydia may at first have missed the musical soirées she had so enjoyed when she first lived with them. But it is clear from the letters we do have that Hugh and Lydia became friendly with many of the best known Edinburgh Free Church Ministers, such as Dr Thomas Guthrie,[23] Dr James Buchanan,[24] Dr Julius Wood[25] and James Noble;[26] that they counted among their friends such medical men as Professor James Miller[27] and J. Y. Simpson.[28] And of course they had friends among the scientists such as Sir David Brewster.[29] So, although Lydia may have been disappointed that those they had met in 1839 who had 'looked upon

23  Thomas Guthrie (1803–1873) studied at Edinburgh and Paris and was Minister of Old Greyfriars in Edinburgh 1837–40, then St John's. He joined the Free Church at the Disruption and was Moderator in 1862. He was a notable preacher and philanthropist.

24  James Buchanan (1804–1870) was Minister of St Giles, Edinburgh in 1840 and joined the Free Church at the Disruption, becoming Minister of Free St Stephen's, Edinburgh. He published many theological works.

25  Julius Wood (1800–1877) was born at Jedburgh and ordained in 1827. He was Minister of the Free Church, Dumfries in 1848, and Moderator in 1857. He obtained his doctorate in 1856. It is not known if he was a connection of Marion Wood's.

26  James Noble (1803–1864) was born at Killearnan near Inverness. He studied classics, philosophy, medicine and theology at King's College, Aberdeen and Edinburgh. Ordained in 1839, he was Minister of the Gaelic Church, Edinburgh at the time of the Disruption, when he joined the Free Church. He was translated to Poolewe in 1849.

27  James Miller (1812–1864) was educated at St Andrews and Edinburgh universities, becoming assistant to the well-known surgeon Robert Liston in 1842, and Surgeon-in-Ordinary to Queen Victoria in 1848.

28  James Young Simpson (1811–1870), son of a baker, was Professor of Midwifery in Edinburgh in 1839, and introduced the use of chloroform in 1847. He was created baronet in 1866.

29  David Brewster (1781–1868) became a licensed preacher in 1802 but abandoned the clerical profession in favour of taking a doctorate in law at St Andrews University. But his interests were really scientific and he became a Fellow of the Royal Society in 1815. He made discoveries in relation to the polarisation of light and invented the kaleidoscope in 1816. Knighted in 1832, he became a supporter of the Disruption and in 1844 Vice-Chancellor of Edinburgh University. He became President of the Royal Society of Edinburgh in 1864.

Hugh as a lion' were not now flocking round them, at least she was not bereft of good company.

Hugh, however, was changing. As Lydia noticed: 'The gulf which separated the life after the year 1840 and that before it was indeed a very wide one. I know not anywhere else an instance of a man being apparently not one individual but two'. In the Cromarty days he had been mild in expression, extremely gentle in manner, his life busy but serene. When the artist who painted Lydia's portrait (Chapter Five) told her that he thought Hugh to be 'a man of the most *infuriated* expression' he had ever seen, she and her friends had thought this comment ridiculously far from reality. Now there was some truth in it: 'No one could be more utterly relentless, it seemed, in his castigation of an opponent, no one more keenly stinging and caustic in the manner of giving it'. Yet, and Lydia was in a position to know, 'the old nature was always there deep down. And it was always the *view*, the *opinion* he really attacked, not the *man*. "If you want me to crush any one," he would say, half in jest and half in earnest, "don't let me see him".' He had taken to going about armed with a pistol, partly perhaps because he so often had to cross unpopulated 'rough' areas on foot after dark, but also perhaps because he had a fear of attack by his enemies, a point well illustrated by an incident related in Bayne's *Life and Letters*. One evening his old friend Robert Carruthers, on a visit from Inverness and not finding him at home in Sylvan Place, went to meet him on his return from *The Witness* office in the High Street. In the dusk Hugh strode past without recognising him. 'There goes that rascally editor of the *Witness*', joked Carruthers. Hugh turned on him with a pistol. Apologising, he explained afterwards that he half expected to be attacked at any moment.

But Dr Chalmers continued to be a welcome, though infrequent, visitor to Sylvan Place. Lydia remembered 'the "apostolic fervour", softened no doubt with fatherly kindness, with which he put his hand on Harriet's golden head and blessed her'. And there was another committed Non-intrusionist, David Maitland Macgill Crichton of Rankeillour, a 'rugged, simple-hearted country gentleman, intrepid in thought and word, sincere beyond the tolerance of guile, impatient of generalship and suspicious of expediency', who became a close family friend. Crichton so admired and loved Hugh that he named him, with his own brothers, as tutor and guardian to his three youngest children.

Meanwhile, however, Hugh's reputation was growing in his preferred field of geology. In 1841 he published what was to become the third most popular of all his works after *Scenes and Legends* and *Schools and Schoolmasters*, entitled *The Old Red Sandstone; or, New Walks in an Old Field.* This brought him praise from the great scientists of the day such as the pre-eminent geologist, Charles Lyell,[30] the brilliant Swiss zoologist, Louis Agassiz (1807–73), who named two fossil fishes after him, and the great Roderick Murchison[31] to whom Hugh had dedicated *The Old Red Sandstone.*

Hugh's contribution to geology in some ways mirrored what he did for the Non-intrusionist cause. By describing his finds with passion in poetic prose, he made the fledgling science both comprehensible and popular. And this in turn did lead to invitations to dinner parties and social occasions from eminent men such as the Duke of Argyll; but Hugh, genuinely shy and deeply suspicious of being 'lionised', refused many of them. It took time to make intimate friends as he had done in Cromarty, and in any case he resented wasting what little spare time he had on what he considered trivialities.

Their son William (Bill) was born on 28 October 1842. Both before and after this Lydia, with little Ha-Ha almost three, was fully occupied with domestic matters. Which was perhaps just as well, since Hugh was even more than usually occupied with the paper in the months leading up to the dramatic gathering in May 1843, attended by Hugh, at which the Deed of Demission was signed by

30　Charles Lyell (1797–1875) was Professor of Geology at King's College, London 1831–33 and President of the Geological Society 1835–36 and 1849–50. He had already published his *Principles of Geology* and other works. He was knighted in 1848 and created first baronet in 1864.

31　Roderick Impey Murchison (1792–1871) became a distinguished geologist after seven years in the army, Fellow of the Royal Society in 1826 and President of the Royal Geographical Society in 1843. He was knighted in 1846, made KCB in 1863 and first baronet in 1866.

474 Ministers of the Church, and the Free Church of Scotland was brought into existence. Hugh, through his views expressed in *The Witness*, had played a significant part in this Disruption and was given a prominent position by D O Hill in his picture of the signing of the Deed of Demission. After this there was less continuous pressure, and Hugh was able, when editorial duties allowed, to travel in search of new copy for the paper and to pursue his geological interests. Lydia, with two small children, could not accompany him; but she was able to visit some of her new friends who had homes outside Edinburgh.

During a tour of the North of Scotland in July 1843, undertaken partly to find out how the infant Free Church was surviving, Hugh was able to spend some time in Cromarty and visit Lydia's mother. From here he wrote to Lydia:

> Think what you may of the matter, dearest, you have no such admirer as your own husband. You would laugh at me as fond and foolish did you know how often I have been thinking of you during the past week, and how much pleasure I have had in writing this scrawl, just because, however trivial my topic, I felt I was conversing on it with you. You were beside me, as now, and I felt the lover as strong in my heart as I did seven years ago. Do you not remember how many hours we used to sit together, and yet how very short they always seemed? Shall we not, dearest, renew these times at our meeting, ere I plunge once more into the stern turmoil of controversy, and be a man of war? We shall have one or two quiet walks together ere we cross the country to Edinburgh.

Such a letter would have been a comfort for Lydia, but it was not the same as being with him, especially when he visited little Eliza's grave to report:

> The little mound is as well marked as it was four years ago, and it is now wrapped over with a mound of rich unbroken turf. The little head-stone bearing your and my name has whitened somewhat under the influence of the weather, and leans slightly to

one side, but there is no other change . . . Poor Liza! The little events of her span-long life rose all before me, from the time that I first felt that I was a father, till I flung myself down in uncontrollable anguish on my bed, a father no longer. The spring in which we lost her was peculiarly a dark time; – but it is over; and Liza still lives, though not with us.

A few days later, writing at seven in the morning, he was again full of love:

You have been my inseparable companion, dearest, since we parted. You were with me last night on the ridge of the hill, looking at all I looked at and feeling all I felt. Do you remember the exquisite evening we passed among the pines on the upper slope of the hill above the cultivated ground, where the hill looks down upon the town and bay? . . . It was early in our acquaintance, – friendship had passed into love, though we had not yet become aware of the fact; but rarely, I suppose, do mere friends manifest the same unwillingness to part that we did that evening. We lingered on till all that was fine in the sunset had disappeared, and found the grey of sea and sky, and the black-ness of fields and wood, quite as agreeable as the many-tinted landscape we had so admired a little before. My own dear Lydia, – it is an advantage to have recollections such as these to summon up.

Lydia had taken Ha-Ha and the baby Bill, now nine months old, and their nursemaid to Arrochar at the head of Loch Long, but she had not been well. 'You will, I trust, get stronger' wrote Hugh, and

by the time I join you, you will be able to accompany me in my walks. You must take especial care and not over-exert yourself, nor walk much in the sun . . . By extending your walks bit by bit as you felt your strength increase, – never exhausting yourself, – never urging exertion past the point at which fatigue is merely an agreeable languor, you could be brought into condition, and made strong enough to travel ten miles per day. My mother, never a strong woman, has travelled at your age thirty miles on a stretch. Only think of all you could do, could you but travel thirty miles! I shall however, be well content if, at our meeting, I find you able to accomplish five. Five would bring us to Loch Lomond together, and take within our range a few of the striking points of Loch Long . . . To say that my chief pleasure, in a ramble devoted to pleasure exclusively, arises from my conversation with you, is not saying too much. My heart is continually turning to you and the two little persons at Arrochar. My home is not a locality, it is not a dwelling; it is you and the little ones.

It is not known if Hugh did join them there.

During the summer of 1845, for the second time, Hugh joined his old Cromarty friend, the Rev John Swanson, in his 'floating manse', the yacht *Betsey*, visiting small communities in the Western Isles. Lydia was by now expecting her third child and Hugh had intended to be back in Edinburgh for the birth; but Bessie arrived early, on 19 June, Hugh getting back only on the 28th. In a letter to a friend in Inverness dated 11 July Lydia wrote:

My dearest Jessy

Much ashamed I am and ought to be for the time which has elapsed since I received your last kind letter without a reply on my part. My health has been since that time extremely delicate and though I do not say that I have been always absolutely unable to write I may say with truth that writing was some-times impossible and generally a burden to me.

I am now anxious to answer at the same time your last and your brother's exceedingly kind invitation to Mr Miller for the ensuing meeting of the Assembly [of the Free Church which took place in Inverness in 1845]. This is the very first time I have had a pen in my hand since the birth of my little one and my recovery has been both dangerous and tedious. I had a high fever and a threatening of inflammation which has since fallen into my right leg in the shape of inflamed veins. The leg case has been I believe a mild one but I am still as helpless as an infant unable to stand on the one foot from weakness and on the other

from [word illegible] that I can only be rolled over from the bed
to the sofa every day . . .

. . . but I am one of those elastic folks who take sudden starts in
the direction of health when people least expect it. So I do not
despair [of attending the Assembly herself].

This letter contains the only specific description we have of any of
Lydia's health problems, and the comment about her sudden recover-
ies becomes particularly significant when considering her illnesses
later in life.

Hugh himself had not been well and had to cancel a proposed visit
to north-west Scotland and Orkney. Instead he travelled in England,
for the first time in his life, during eight weeks in the autumn of
1845,[32] leaving Lydia and the children in a temporary home in
Archibald Place in Edinburgh. From Birmingham on 5 October he
wrote to Lydia: 'Now, for the last month I have felt, with regard to
my health, as if the "tide was on the turn;" I have been rallying
slowly, but not decisively; and until I feel the flood-stream of health
setting fairly in, I hold it would scarce be justice to you, myself, or
the bairns to return to Archibald Place and commence my labours
with but the prospect of sinking under them'. But he had some
regard also for Lydia's health:

It grieves me to hear that there is still something radically
wrong with your constitution. You must lose no time in getting
to Gifford [where her brother Thomas was now Free Church
minister] . . .

You speak, dearest, of temperament, and the difficulty of
bearing up against it by any mere effort of the will when it is
adverse to small but not unimportant everyday duties. I know
somewhat of that difficulty from experience in myself; willing
may do much, but it will not change nature, or convert uphill
work into downhill. But I trust we shall both get on, bearing
and forbearing, with a solid stratum of affection at bottom. I

32  It was on this trip that Hugh gathered the material for his delightful book
*First Impressions of England and Its People*, published in 1847.

have been conscious since my late attack [a reference to his respiratory lung ailment, a relic of his stonemason days] of an irritability of temper, which is, I hope, not natural to me, and which, when better health comes, will, I trust disappear. I keep it down so that it gives no external sign; since I entered England it has found no expression whatever; but I am very sensible of it, especially after passing a rather sleepless night. Today I am in a very genial humour, the entire secret of which is in the excellence of last night's rest, induced, I think, by the fatigue of the previous day. I mention the thing merely in corroboration of your remark; – we cannot be independent of the animal part of us.

In an undated letter from Birmingham Hugh revealed that this visit to England, although interesting in many ways, was not really helping him to recover his spirits:

You have often told me that I set a higher value on mere existence than you do, – that with reference to human creatures in general I think less of suffering and more of death, and I daresay I have thought to reply, – whether I have said it or not, – 'alas wife, you are a Celt and I am a Saxon [although he was in fact descended from Highlanders through his maternal grandmother], and Celts are prodigal of life as all know.' But believe me, dearest, however great my respect for life which once spilled cannot be gathered, my mere existence has no charms for myself, and if it was not for you and the bairns I would care little how soon my head were down. You are my anchor and must give me a kindly tug just to let me know that I am not drifting from land.

It is clear that Lydia and Hugh never had any difficulty in communicating their feelings to each other. But Hugh, despite his reference to the weakness in her constitution only two weeks earlier, wrote to her (she had evidently not gone to Gifford) on 16 October:

By the way, if this reach you ere you have left the north, I would suggest to you coming south by the omnibus that plies from

Fort William to Loch Lomond, – passing through Glencoe and the Deer Forest of Breadalbane. You would see by this means some of the wildest scenery in the kingdom, – scenery that ere the establishment of the present conveyance was scarcely accessible to ladies at all, and to men only at a considerable expense of money and exertion. It would be well for you to secure an inside seat, with the stipulation that you might if you like ride outside. Glencoe is often drenched by deluging rains, and if you took merely an outside seat, – by far the most advantageous for sight-seeing, – you might suffer as much as you did in the storm of Loch Katrine.

We do not know where Lydia was, but she had Harriet not yet six with her, and even without the child such a journey would probably have been more than she could undertake, however much she would have wished to. It is likely that she returned south by sea, always her preferred mode of travel.

Early in 1846 the family moved to a house in Stuart Street, just outwith the City limits, for which the rent was 'something over £30 a year' and made Hugh liable to 'half-year taxes'. This appears to have been one of four houses just off the Portobello Road, probably where Abercorn Gardens now is beside Piershill Cemetery. Hugh believed that being thus 'quite in the country' was good for the health and enjoyment of the children, who had been suffering from the whooping cough and measles. He himself benefited from the daily walk of two or three miles (depending on the route he chose) to *The Witness* offices; but on the nights when the paper went to press he could not always return home, instead staying the night with his half-brother, Andrew Williamson, who was now employed by the newspaper.

Being further out from the centre of Edinburgh, with Hugh not always able to get home at the end of his day's work, Lydia may have found life less stimulating, particularly intellectually. Her compensation was having more time to write – and this was when she turned from writing books for children, of which she had already published three, to tackling a novel.

# NINE

# Lydia the Writer

Many Scottish women in the Victorian era took to writing novels and children's stories, usually moral and didactic, often to bring in extra money. As Lydia matured she needed – as Hugh had rightly advised when they were courting – some intellectual occupation for her mind. She had found this in writing for the annuals before her marriage and thereafter occasional book reviews for *The Witness* in the early years of Hugh's editorship, also in helping him compose his leading articles on Church matters. After the Disruption, she wanted to develop this talent. It cannot have been easy to find time for this while running a household with small children, even when her mother came to stay and help; and the moves to Archibald Place and Stuart Street must have been disruptive. But she did manage to write four books for children published in 1845 and 1846. This, however, was not enough. She had been fired with as much enthusiasm for the birth of the Free Church in 1843 as Hugh, and she decided to tackle a far more ambitious task – to spread the message to an English readership by encapsulating the essence of the Disruption in a novel. The result was the publication in 1847 of *Passages in the Life of an English Heiress, or Recollections of Disruption Times in Scotland.*

This was an enormous challenge, to put the case for the Disruption, to set the Free Church in a social context and try to make it acceptable not only to the Moderates in Scotland but also to readers in England; to explain and justify in fiction what had been done in fact. It had to cover not only the facts of the Disruption itself, but the background of Patronage and the intrusion of unsuitable Ministers. But she had to have regard for the evangelical outlook of her Church, which considered that fiction was 'simply a lie and as such intrinsically immoral ... Fiction corrupted the reader, it inflamed the passions and made vice interesting'. So her romantic imagination had to be restricted.

Earlier women novelists – Maria Edgeworth,[33] Susan Ferrier,[34] even at times Jane Austen – wrote of ingenuous heroines who retained their innate 'goodness' despite being exposed to scenes of 'passion and vice' such as married women eloping with depraved lovers, reckless spending, deceit, duels and debauchery. The Brontë sisters, Charlotte, Emily and Anne, published their first and dramatic novels, *Jane Eyre, Wuthering Heights* and *Agnes Grey,* in the same year, 1847, as Lydia published hers. First novels by subsequent prolific and important women authors, who did take a more moral tone and described social problems, were published after Lydia's and included *Mary Barton* by Mrs Gaskell (1848), *Passages in the Life of Margaret Maitland,* which also touched on the Disruption, by Mrs Oliphant (1849), Harriet Beecher Stowe's anti-slavery *Uncle Tom's Cabin* (1851-52), and *The Heir of Radclyffe* by Charlotte Yonge (1853). But Lydia had to avoid 'the excitements' of the earlier writers and so her novel lacked their popular appeal. Moreover, the severity of her strictures on patronage, intrusion and the Highland clearances would have angered some of the 'Moderates' and the landed class. Her novel, therefore, was not a great success. It was published anonymously in London by Richard Bentley and there must have been enough sales to justify its reissue a few months later by Simpkin, Marshall & Co. But it seems to have disappeared completely apart from a copy in the British Library and one tattered copy in the National Library of Scotland in Edinburgh.

The plot follows the life of Jane Hamilton Legh. Her late father, Sir Arthur, was a baron and Member of Parliament, with an estate in the English Midlands and Whig tendencies, but who had 'found no party with whom to cooperate heartily'. He had taught Jane that wealth and land bring duties towards tenants, not because of religious morality but on the basis of ethics. She had a mind 'naturally strong and

33  Maria Edgeworth (1768–1849), daughter of a wealthy Irish landowner.
34  Susan Ferrier (1787–1854), wife of an Edinburgh lawyer.

reflective, . . . [which had] . . . imbibed a more vigorous tone of thinking than is usual with her sex; her sensibilities, however, were cast in a more delicate mould than those of many who threw a sneer at her pursuits as being of too masculine a character'. Her mother had been the sister of a northern baronet, whose estate, Rosemount, lay in the western part of Ross-shire. Lydia was as proud as any Highlander of her mother's connection to the Mackenzies of Redcastle and her close ancestral links to the great Highland clans of Mackintosh, Macleod and Fraser.

At a dinner party at this northern estate Jane is teased for studying politics and reading Harriet Martineau, the philosopher and advocate of social reform whose attempt to popularise economic subjects through fiction may have given Lydia the idea of doing the same for Evangelical theology.[35] Jane learns of the 'controversy between the reforming and the anti-reforming clergy' in Scotland and one of the lairds present suggests that the Moderates 'have something more of the gentlemen about them . . . they don't meddle with what does not concern them . . . they can sing a good song, take a hand at whist, and, in short, be friendly and social in their way: and then you know it is natural that, after all that, they should tip the wink at certain gentle-manly follies'. Jane asks to be pardoned if she thinks 'those accomplishments you have mentioned are not the chief ends of a clergyman's life'.

The subject then turns to morality. The laird considers 'morality a disagreeable sort of word. I think it should be banished from polite society . . . "Oh yes," said one of the Misses Grant, "I think it so stiff and formal". "Quite old-maidenish," said one of the Misses Fraser. "I think," said Mrs Grant, who was considered a sensible woman, "that young ladies should not meddle with things which it is not to be

---

35 Harriet Martineau (1802–1876), a Unitarian, suffered much illness and by 1829 was almost destitute despite having had some articles printed and short stories published. But after this, especially after coming to London and travelling to America and other countries, she successfully published books on economic subjects, and a novel, *Deerbrook*, in 1839. She continued writing successfully until her death.

expected they can understand." "Unless they want to be called blue stockings," said Mrs Fraser, a little spitefully".'

This conversation could have come straight from an Edinburgh tea-party. To be labelled bluestocking was certainly no compliment. As we have seen, Hugh had been careful to write to Lydia that in spite of her intellectual powers she was no such thing.

Next the discussion turns to patronage, which is at the root of the novel. Dr Blair, the local minister, is about to retire. The congregation wants to be free to choose his successor, but Jane's 'mad-cap' young cousin Harry, patron of the living, has promised it to the unpopular profligate son of an even more unpopular local minister called Donaldson. The pro-patronage, pro-intrusion cause is put bluntly by a local laird. Peasants, he considers, are not capable of choosing their own ministers. "The long and the short of it is, Miss Legh . . . that the Church may go to the bottom, before I lose my patronages . . . I tell you, there's not a boor of them shall get living of mine without pledging himself against this non-intrusion humbug." (Lydia, however, has Jane's influence on this cousin, wounded in the first Afghan War, leading to his writing to her from his deathbed in Kabul to show that he has become a reformed character.)

These then are the basic themes of Lydia's novel: a church in need of reformation and a journey back to 'its original purity', a church no longer contaminated by the Moderatism of the landowners and their tame clergymen intruded by the ungodly act of patronage. An ambitious theme, certainly, but one which Lydia was well placed to handle. She would have been aware of all classes of opinion both in the Highlands and in Edinburgh during the late 1830s and early '40s. Her handling of the dinner-party conversation is skilful and rings true.

After this introduction Lydia takes us first to a humble cottage where an old lay preacher, tended by his twelve-year-old granddaughter May, is dying. He tells May how soldiers sent to intrude the ungodly minister, Donaldson, into the local parish shot her mother. Then to the other local parish where the revered but ailing minister, Dr Blair, is about to hold his last Communion service. Some fine descriptive writing follows the arrival of the parishioners from miles around on a beautiful April morning, the sort of scene Lydia must herself have witnessed, perhaps on her visit to the parish of Urquhart in the Black Isle under the charismatic John MacDonald (Chapter Five). And Dr Blair's pious and emotional sermon, given in full, is an amalgam of those she must have heard preached countless times.

There are other vignettes before Jane, on the eve of going to Edinburgh, takes a walk in the mountains. Lydia knew well the area she describes so effectively. Jane climbs high into a

tumultuous sea of heathy mountains, which stretched on inter-minable, as it appeared towards the north. Over their vast barrenness, their brown and naked sterility, silence and solitude reigned undisturbed. Ridge within ridge heaved themselves upwards, as if the long rolling waves of an ocean of molten land had been transfixed in their gigantic swell by the hand of Omnipotence . . . A light mist had begun to creep up the bases of the hills. At first, thin as the web of the gossamer, it reflected the rays of the sun, and served merely to add softness to the landscape. Almost insensibly, like the change in a diorama, it rolled itself as it stole upwards into fantastic wreaths, and transformed the rugged features of the mountain scenery into those of varied gracefulness and beauty. Then deepening in volume and gathering into dark clouds, with edges of silver, it came rapidly and more rapidly onwards, until the tops of the mountains, still shining clear in the sun-light, looked like islands in the midst of an ocean of clouds.

Jane recalls the tales of Fingal and Ossian, the heroes of Celtic song 'till as she looked upwards, she almost expected to see the faces of "the warriors of other days looking from their clouds".'

We are next taken to Edinburgh where Jane stays with aristo-cratic cousins, the Earl and Countess of Lentraethen and their daughters, the Ladies Grace and Emily Maitland, who are amiable, sophisticated but mentally lazy, disliking 'all that was obtrusively offensive in temper or disposition, as they would have disliked an unpleasant taste or smell . . . Good to them was a surface thing, a matter of little more than mere taste; with their cousin it was earnest, serious – her chief end of living'. At a dinner party with a great Tory aristocrat, Sir Charles Murray, she notes that Edinburgh ladies are less soft and polished than their English counterparts. They use a harsher language unlike the 'exquisite harmony in tones and movements of highly educated English women'. On the other hand Scottish women are more frank and inclined to think for themselves.

Conversation turns to the question of the 'non-intrusionist agitators' and the names of Dr Candlish and Dr Chalmers are raised. Jane however asks too many questions and goes too far. "Don't become a Non-intrusionist", she is urged: "It's bad enough to be a Whig." But there is another guest at the dinner-table, Lord Lentraethen's brother, General Frederick Maitland. Sir Charles apologises to him for introducing the subject for 'he is an avowed advocate of the Non-intrusionist party'.

After dinner the General and Jane enter into a long discussion on the subject of patronage in general and in the Church of England as opposed to the Church of Scotland. Here one can almost hear the voices of Hugh and Lydia in earnest discussion of the various issues of the day, batting the ball of patronage and intrusion back and forth as if to clarify their own minds. But this anxiety to preach and explain leads Lydia to produce a long-winded polemical dialogue which should have been broken up into more digestible sections. Nor is it necessary. By her vivid portrayal of Highland parish life she conveys her message far more effectively, such as in her description of the attempt to intrude the odious Donaldson. This is obviously based on the Resolis riot of 28 September 1843, caused by the intrusion of an unpopular replacement for the Reverend Donald Sage, during which a woman was arrested and then rescued from the cell in the Cromarty Courthouse by the rioters, who invaded Lydia's mother's garden in the process.

Jane, although finding the handsome General Maitland a stimulating partner for a serious discussion of church issues, and although encouraged by her young cousins to 'captivate' him, can only see him as a rather cold old bachelor ten years her senior. She discovers, however, that he had been married 'to one of those baby-wives that are so common in India; a very lovely toy . . . but expensive' and that he has a daughter, Julia. 'The door flew open, and the bright eyes of one of the loveliest children Jane had ever seen looked eagerly around the room for her papa; and in a moment she was locked in his arms. The little external frost-work of the General's manner instantly gave way, as once and again the child hung on his neck and hid her face in his bosom.' She now realised that 'he was one of those characters who endeavour to hide great tenderness of heart, and a deeply wounded sensibility, under a slight appearance of external coldness and reserve'. Jane is painfully reminded of her own loss of a father. ' "You must forgive me General Maitland," said she, endeavouring to smile. "This child reminds me irresistibly of – of twelve years ago; – and you know," she added, her expression changing into that of deep sorrow, "my dress is still mourning!" ' The General falls in love.

Here surely is Lydia deliberately recalling how she at first had no thought of marrying Hugh, also ten years her senior, and his devotion to little Eliza. And her sense of social justice is brought out when she has the General telling her that his aims as a landlord are threefold: to improve the soil for the sake of his tenants and himself, to see that the physical well-being of his tenants is as high as he can make it, but more important to improve their spiritual well-being 'by looking to the condition of my own soul in order to promote the spiritual welfare of the others'.

Jane is introduced to Dr Chalmers, and it is interesting that Lydia, who of course knew him, chooses to emphasise that aspect of his appearance that concerned her so much in Hugh, his clothing. 'Simplicity pervaded every movement, and even communicated itself . . . to the very dress which he wore. His clothes sat upon him without slovenliness, yet so plainly to indicate that they were no part of himself; that they had never in the course of his life cost him an anxiety or care. The folds of his neckcloth, and the very tie upon it, without an indication of eccentricity told of a toilet devoid of concentration . . . But there was a charm in this simplicity quite beyond the reach of imitation. Miss Legh was struck too with the remarkable beauty, as well as the size of his head . . . ' Here is a portrait both of Chalmers and of Hugh.

Lydia gives a vivid description of Jane attending the General Assembly of the Church of Scotland of 1841, at which seven Moderate ministers in the presbytery of Strathbogie were deposed, despite an interdict of the Court of Session. She has the General answering Jane's questions, and commenting on the issues, with Hugh's voice: 'A pure heart cannot rest in iniquity – a pure Church cannot rest in impurity; and while there are so many hostile forces brought to bear outwardly and inwardly on Christians and Churches, how shall there be rest complete and absolute? It will come – on earth comparatively – in heaven consummately'.

From here on Lydia does allow herself to introduce romance, and even some fantasies. The General proposes and Jane accepts. They go to visit Jane's English estate and her late father is portrayed as a god-like figure who in his lifetime had created and governed an earthly paradise. The land is fertile, the cottages festooned in roses and honeysuckle. There is employment for all. The interests of landlord and tenant are of mutual benefit. Jane tells her husband, 'My father said he was determined to banish pauperism and misery from at least one estate in old England. . . . "Ah!" replies the general, "would that we had a nation of such legislators as Sir Arthur!" '

The General is elevated on the death of his brother to the Earldom and Jane finds herself Countess of Lentraethen. He returns to take control of his Scottish estate, leaving his bride to take a closer look at her earthly paradise of Chesterlee. This gives Lydia the opportunity to include in her novel a message for her English readers about the state of their Church, to call on them to emulate the Scots and get rid of patronage, state control and, in their case, the insidious influence of papacy. The Oxford Movement, which had arisen from John Keble's 1833 sermon on National Apostasy, had published a series of tracts which asserted among other things that the Church of England was not simply an Establishment subject to the will of Parliament. It was a true branch of the Church Catholic, under the sole headship of Christ and reflecting the purity of the original apostolic Church. This, however, had led to High Church ritual. And many saw in this 'Popish practices' and infiltration by Roman Catholics.

There were already, at the time when Lydia was writing, stories going the rounds of the introduction into English parishes of clergy who in fact were secret Jesuit converts. Lydia may even have heard such stories from her Egham relations, and it was only seven years after her novel was published, in 1854, that the Jesuit Father Clarke, disguising himself as a farmer, managed secretly to buy Beaumont close to Windsor Great Park which later became a Jesuit College. But she has her heroine Jane discovering that, after the death of her father and the incumbent of the local parish, the land-steward had *sold* the living. Not only was this quite contrary to the long practice of the lords of the manor 'that their church-patronage had been unsullied by purchases', it had in fact been sold to a secret Jesuit who was introducing High Church rituals. Jane's father had always said that there was 'no parleying with despotism . . . no country can flourish with Rome politically or morally'. She herself objects to what she sees as 'a race of degraded and enslaved priests reared to enslave and degrade mankind'. And both she and her husband had decided that if 'the plague spot of Popery in their own backyard spreads any further, they will try to form a Free Church of England . . . unfettered by State support'.

Lydia was here reflecting the anti-Popish attitude of Hugh and many of his Free Church associates, an intolerance just as stubborn as that which she sought to condemn. But it was a mistake to interrupt in this way the flow of her explanation for English readers of the Disruption in Scotland, which then continues, effectively, with her description of the scene on 18 May 1843 when nearly five hundred ministers walked out of the Assembly Hall of St Andrew's to form the First Assembly of the Free Church of Scotland in Tanfield Hall. We are all witnesses as they sign the Act of Separation and Deed of Demission under the Moderatorship of Dr Chalmers. As the whole congregation rise to sing the psalm 'Oh send thy light forth and thy truth; let them be guides to me', at that moment in true dramatic style, 'the sun, beclouded for a time, streams in with unusual brightness, and illuminates the open Bible'.

After this Jane rejoins her husband to take over the estate of Rosemount, which has been left to her by her uncle. She finds it heavily encumbered with debt, and that many of the former tenants have been victims of the Clearances. This gives Lydia the context for an effective diatribe on this 'evil', a subject to which Hugh devoted much space in *The Witness* in 1846 and 1847, with Jane restoring them to their properties and the evil Donaldson being replaced with a minister of the congregation's choice.

Lydia should have left it there, but she concludes with a romantic and improbable description of her return, with her husband, to Chesterlee, and the birth of their child who lies like a young god 'in his cradle of mother-of-pearl, shaped like the shell of a nautilus, and sculptured all over; an exquisite piece of art, in which the young Lord Arthur lay sleeping; its silken curtain so disposed as to shade his little face from the light, and yet to permit his mother's eye to rest on it on her first awakening'.

So what are we to make of this long and uneven work? The book would have been easier to read if only Lydia had known how to edit it. She demonstrates that she was well able to sustain a plot, create credible characters and handle scenery. There is some excellent descriptive writing and every so often a touch of humour to enliven the heavier scenes. She makes good use of her knowledge of Edinburgh and English county society. It was a bold and brave attempt to fulfil its mission, to get acceptance of the social significance of the Free Church.

No review of this novel in England has been found. It may have been Hugh who wrote the review which appeared in *The Witness* of 1 January 1848. It ran to nearly four thousand words and treated the book with proper respect. After apologising for the delay in printing a critique, the reviewer makes the point that 'there are cases in which the novel may be the best vehicle for conveying instruction; and we are also persuaded that the subject of this work is to unfold the causes and character of the Disruption, especially to the English mind'. This being the aim of the book, 'the conception of the work was not more happy than its execution is successful'.

The reviewer makes only one tentative criticism: 'There is,

especially at the opening of scenes, a want of artistic arrangement; and now and then a slight formality of style; but these are very minor matters, and may, with a little trouble, be corrected in future editions'. The rest however is glory: 'The peculiarity of the work we have not yet attested to. We refer to the original and profound observations both on the subject of human life, and on the special question discussed, scattered throughout the work, so numerous as to occur on every page and which take the reader by surprise, and, more than anything else, impress him with a sense of the writer's powers'.

This last phrase at least is true. Although flawed in so many ways, Lydia's book demonstrates both talent and potential. All the way through one catches glimpses of just how good a writer lurked behind the facade of evangelical fervour and the need to preach. It is a pity that she did not – as far as is known – attempt another adult novel. But she did continue to write for children, and after Hugh's death she applied her talents as a writer to great effect in editing his posthumous works (Chapter Thirteen).

We know of seventeen books for children written by her. Most sold well, many going into several editions, even after her own death. And the fact that some of them were even written in the very early years of her widowhood, and while she was heavily occupied with Hugh's posthumous works, shows how important writing was to her. With one exception, all were published under the pseudonym Harriet Myrtle, and they show Lydia's undoubted talent for teaching small children, and an understanding of how to keep their interest, as well as her eagerness to instil in them all the Christian virtues.

In *A Story Book of Country Scenes*, published by Routledge in 1846, she says: 'The object of these stories of country life is to awaken in the minds of young children a taste for simple pleasures and active duties . . . the author has sought to point out to her little readers God's goodness, as manifested in the beauties and pleasures of each several seasons of the year, and also to inspire them with a tender and humane care for the living creatures He has bestowed upon them'. Like Hugh she wanted her readers to examine and enjoy the works of nature. All her books for children are in true Victorian tradition, intended to teach and preach. But the themes and settings are full of variety.

In *The Man of Snow*, for example, published in 1848, there is a black footman portrayed with both humour and affection who manages to get the better of local inhabitants. The book shows no trace of jingoism or racial superiority. Similarly there is an Indian ayah in one of the stories in *Home and its Pleasures*, published in 1852, who behaves far better than her English fellow servants. *Amusing Tales*, published in 1853, teaches the responsibilities of the 'upper classes' towards the 'lower classes': it includes a story of gypsies accused wrongly of doing damage until the guilty boy – one of the gentry – owns up and the gypsies are fairly treated. *The Little Foundling and Other Stories* (the title refers to a baby sparrow) includes detailed instructions and a diagram for making a kite, and suggests that Hugh may have found time from his editorial duties to make one for William. *A Visit to the New Forest*, published in 1859, is a lively and educational book, containing history, geography and nature lessons. It introduces readers to Ivanhoe and Robin Hood, includes a good deal of adventure, and suggests games to play on wet days. Place names such as Broadstairs and Ramsgate are mentioned with such confidence that it is obvious that Lydia herself must have visited them, possibly when she was living at Egham Lodge.

Scotland is the background, either by implication or directly, to several. *Always Do Your Best and Lizzie Lindsay*, another published in 1859, features in the first story a somewhat wild boy looked after by his grandmother, who suffers from rheumatism. Lydia may have taken her plot from events in Hugh's childhood. Lizzie Lindsay – the name seems to have been taken from a popular traditional Scottish song (*Leezie Lindsay*) of the period which Lydia probably sang to her own family – is the granddaughter of a surly but repentant Scottish laird.

*Aunt Maddy's Diamonds*, set in Fife and published in 1864, is a moral story featuring Fanny who hates a fairy tale about a girl who found frogs coming out of her mouth when she was naughty. 'Some wise people now-a-days object to fairy tales, but Aunt Maddy had a great fancy for them, thinking that a useful lesson was often contained in them.' Fanny soon realises that when she is naughty Aunt Maddy sees "frogs coming out of her mouth" but at the end of the tale, when she has learned better behaviour, Aunt Maddy sees diamonds.

*Cats and Dogs, Nature's Warriors and God's Workers: or Mrs Myrtle's Lessons in Natural History* (published in 1857 with the author's name given simply as L.F.F.M.) was the most successful of her books, with second and third editions appearing in 1868 and 1872; and not long before her death in 1876 Lydia must have been working on a revised edition, for it was turned into two separate books, *The Dog and his Cousins, the Wolf, the Jackal and the Hyena* appearing, probably post-humously, in 1876, and *Stories of the Cat, and her Cousins the Lion, the Tiger, etc* in 1877. A copy of the second edition of *Cats and Dogs*, now subtitled *Notes and Anecdotes of Two Great Families of the Animal Kingdom* and published by Nelson, is preserved in the Hugh Miller Cottage in Cromarty, and is particularly interesting for its clear connection with that town and Lydia's own background.

The story is about two children, Bessie and Harry Myrtle, who live 'in a very good house situated in a village near the sea-coast' with their governess, parents, elder brother Arthur, who is studying for the ministry, and elder sister Marjory, who plays the piano. The story opens just before Christmas. The children have been 'dressed for dinner' and are waiting with their mamma in the drawing room for the bell to ring for dinner. But their papa is late, 'so mamma said they must wait on for another half-hour'. How often that must have happened in the Miller household! In fact papa is a shadowy but honoured figure throughout.

The book begins with a lengthy history of the cat, from the purpose of its bodily organs to its religious importance in ancient Egypt. Nothing is left out. From household cats the story moves on to describe all members of the cat family from the lion to the lynx. Dogs are treated similarly, from the pet to the wolf. There are detailed line drawings throughout and Lydia shows just how well she knows her subject. But she steers a delicate course between the natural instincts of animals (without souls) to be cruel to each other simply as a means to survival, and the legitimate need of man (with a soul) having to kill for food, when it should be done as humanely as possible.

Interestingly, in the guise of Mrs Myrtle, Lydia tells the children how 'my papa used to amuse me greatly by telling me many stories of the days and weeks he had once been accustomed to spend in following red-deer on the Highland hills', and goes on to describe in some detail the art of deer-stalking (which she must have heard from her father, once 'famous in Strathnairn as a deer-stalker'), emphasising the skill needed and the purpose of providing food. But also, after describing the hunting of deer with dogs, she writes, in a passage which would not be out of place in today's bitter arguments:

> Once on a time there was a real necessity for clearing the country of wolves, and bears, and foxes. Hunting required courage and manhood and was then a noble sport. If it is honestly pursued for the sake of the venison, we may call it a fine sport still; but what shall we say of the practice of letting a poor stag go loose, after it has endured all the fatigue and terror of the chase, in order that it may be hunted again and again, many times over! Is not that at once cowardly and cruel?

The book is full of the strong religious dogma of the day. Through Mrs Myrtle she continually emphasises the point that animals were created and designed by God primarily for the use of mankind. The horse, for example, was fashioned for transport, the camel to help man survive in the desert, the sheep to provide food and clothing. 'All creatures manifest the eternal thought and the eternal will. Their physical conformity displays the unfailing harmony which is demonstrated in all the works of the Creator.' The book ends with an instruction to be kind to animals, for they were made by God, but always to remember that man is superior in that he has a soul. 'Why should we, who, like the inferior animals are born, eat and die, deny them our sympathies, or refuse to acknowledge that in their lives and instincts, God manifests mysterious depths of wisdom and know-ledge . . . On the other hand, dear children, let us remember that God made us only a little lower than the angels; that he has crowned us with glory and honour in giving us those souls, which are within us, the incorruptible germs of an immortal life.'

Whatever we may think of these sentiments today, Lydia was reflecting the beliefs of the Victorian Church in general, and of the Free Church of Scotland and Hugh in particular. The treatment of Mrs Myrtle's relationship with her children strikes us as sentimental, but again it is merely a reflection of the children's literature of the age: Queen Victoria's childhood reading list contained many such books. What does come over strongly is Lydia's ability to teach. She knows her subject thoroughly and it is evident that she enjoyed communicating that knowledge to her young readers. She displays a lively imagination, good dialogue, the ability to create and sustain a plot and an understanding and love of children. She also displays a strong interest in and knowledge of flora and fauna. Her settings are wide and varied and she includes references to train, coach and sea journeys in England based on her own experiences. Although there is no underlying vein of humour, there is plenty of fun and tricks that would make children laugh.

Had it not been for the later tragedy in her life, Lydia might well have developed her writing career to greater heights. She might have produced a fine novel, perhaps more than one, and might also be remembered today as a nineteenth-century children's writer in the style of Mrs Molesworth, Frances Crompton or Catherine Moreland.

# Ten Difficult Years

Despite the success of *First Impressions,* 1847 was not a good year for Hugh. He was now co-proprietor of *The Witness* with Mr Fairly. The paper was flourishing, perhaps because he had made it in many ways unconventional for an Evangelical church newspaper. He filled it with such diverse topics as American Slavery, Destitution in the Highlands and The Gospel in Turkey. At the same time, however, he did not neglect matters of direct relevance to the Free Church. In 1846, for instance, he had included an article on the Free Church Education Scheme and, significantly, articles on Four Letters of Dr Candlish and on Sabbath Observance. But he was having trouble with the Free Church and Dr Candlish in particular.

After the heady days of the Disruption, when so much money was needed to build new churches and schools, and sustain new ministers and schoolmasters, promised subscriptions to the school building fund were beginning to dry up. So Candlish instigated a dynamic programme for restoring what he called the 'old Scottish association of religion and learning'. Hugh was not in favour. As D R Withrington put it in his contribution to *Scotland in the Age of the Disruption,* he thought 'the scheme had an awkward sacerdotal, even Jesuitical, flavour', that Candlish was 'bent on subjecting teachers to clerical domination' and that this would discourage prospective teachers from coming forward.

This naturally upset Candlish who in any case had begun to disapprove of Hugh's style of editorship, particularly what he called Hugh's lack of 'taste, tact and delicacy'. He tried to persuade Fairly that he should replace Hugh, who should be bought off. Fairly informed Hugh, who was in Cromarty at the time. He was furious and immediately penned a 10,000-word letter to, as Bayne put it, 'the

Committee of gentlemen who had from the first interested themselves in the paper, repelling attacks of which he believed himself to be the object'. Near the end of this letter he wrote: 'I have been an honest journalist. During the seven years in which I have edited the *Witness,* I have never once given expression to an opinion which I did not conscientiously regard as sound, nor stated a fact which, at the time at least, I did not believe to be true. My faults have no doubt been many; but they have not been faults of principle; nor have they lost me the confidence of the portion of the people of Scotland to which I belong, and which I represent'. Whether Candlish got wind of this is not clear, but before it could be delivered to the Committee, he, who was of course a member, sent a note to Hugh, now back in Edinburgh, to say that his interference had been misunderstood and he wished it to be regarded as not having taken place. Hugh, however, went ahead, delivering his letter to the Committee in mid-January 1847, where, with the backing of Dr Chalmers, he was completely vindicated.

This event did not become public until after Hugh's death. The paper continued to flourish, but it was a bitter triumph for Hugh. Bayne wrote: 'The independence of the journal had been vindicated, once and for ever; the clergy never came near *The Witness* Office; but, after all, it was isolation rather than independence that was attained, and there was a gaunt and desolate feeling about it. What it must have been to Hugh Miller is not easy to realise'.

To make matters worse, his two great friends and protagonists, Dr Chalmers and the Reverend Alexander Stewart, both died later that year, leaving the field wide open to Candlish and his supporters. Hugh probably felt that he had been betrayed by the ministers of his beloved Free Church. It did not stop him continuing to handle Free Church matters in the paper; but he also offered more scope in its columns for the expression of opinion by rival factions while, as Donald Macleod wrote in *Hugh Miller and the Controversies of Victorian Science,* he 'focussed on the outside world and poured forth a brilliantly sustained series of editorials on science, literature, politics, history, theology and social affairs. That was what sold *The Witness* and that was why the Free Church continued to command respect and attention'.

It would have been surprising if Hugh's troubles had not had some effect on the marriage. He was becoming somewhat embittered and this, combined with his reluctance to get involved in what he called the time-wasting trivialities of social life, may have had its effect on Lydia. She had her hands full domestically. She was herself not in the best of health, and Hugh was so immersed in his work that there must have been few opportunities for them to spend quiet times together.

Lydia at least had her own friends, from her schooldays in Inverness, from her time in Cromarty and now in Edinburgh. From the Woods and Nobles, despite their removal so soon to Dumfries and Poolewe respectively, and from the Buchanans she always had the closest support and help. In a letter to Harriet Ross there is particular mention of an Eliza Borthwick 'whose friendship indeed I reckon of a signal mercy of God and one of the greatest blessings I possess'. Also the youngest Flyter daughter, 'Aunt Ronalda' to the Miller children, was running a small school in Edinburgh. And Harriet Ross mentions in her *Recollections* that Catherine Allardyce was one of Lydia's close friends. But, despite his many preoccupations, Hugh did not neglect her or the family. Marion Wood in her *Recollections* recalls that once towards the end of 1848, when calling on Lydia, she heard that Hugh was giving 'some little lectures on geology to a few lady friends' at their house on Saturday afternoons, to which she was then invited, and that these meetings 'frequently ended by our enjoying Mrs Miller's hospitality and society at luncheon' when she was able to witness Hugh's gentle manner to his family and various demonstrations of his strong parental love. Lydia herself could sometimes escape from Edinburgh, although without Hugh, for instance visiting her brother Thomas, Free Church minister in Gifford, who married Caroline Neale in 1849. And she also turned to charitable works.

The few surviving letters from Lydia to Harriet Ross bear no indication of the year in which they were written (nor, even, in most cases the month); but one dated only November 14th was obviously written during the period of the Irish potato famines which had begun in 1845 and spread next year to the Highlands of Scotland.

Harriet was then in Cromarty recovering from some illness and Lydia was appealing for help in charitable work:

> Having just got up after a week of severe illness I would not write you at present but that I have a little favour to ask & that it is indispensable to its accomplishment that it should not be delayed. I have been applied to for work to be sold in Belfast for the benefit of the poor starving or rather *dying* Irish under the auspices of Dr Edgar a well known Presbyterian clergyman. Having a good needlewoman in the nursery I mean Dr E to have some things made to send over & it would be obliging me very much if *your sister* [Mary] would send me in a letter some trifles or baubles to help my box. Perhaps too some of my other young friends ... would kindly send me something which I would consider as sent to myself. You may perhaps hear it remarked that labour would be better bestowed on the poor *Highlanders.* Most cheerfully will I give my labour & all the material I can spare for these too & surely *young* people enjoying all the comforts of life may give some of that employment to which they often have recourse for their own amusement to save from a dreadful death a few of these fellow creatures whether they be *Irish* or *Highland.*

Such admirable sentiments were part of Lydia's make-up. There was a widespread feeling in the Lowlands, which Hugh strongly criticised in articles in *The Witness* in the last few months of 1846, that the Highlanders' problems sprang from their own idleness and deserved little sympathy. This was perhaps why an appeal for help for the Irish rather than for the Highlanders had come Lydia's way. But, as is clear from her novel, Lydia certainly did not share this view and obviously wanted to make this clear to Harriet.

Hugh was in Cromarty at the time and knew of this appeal, for in a letter to Lydia from there dated 15 December he wrote:

> By the way, how comes it that it is for the *Irish* the Edinburgh ladies are exerting themselves? The Irish are, to be sure, human creatures, but they are human creatures of a considerably lower

order than the Scotch Highlanders, who are at least suffering as much; and they have surely not such a claim on the Scotch. They will be better cared for, too. They are buying guns, and will be by-and-by shooting magistrates and clergymen by the score; and Parliament will in consequence do a great deal for them. But the poor Highlanders will shoot no one, not even a site-refusing laird or a brutal factor, and so they will be left to perish unregarded in their hovels. I see more and more every day the philosophy of Cobbet's advice to the chopsticks of Kent, "if you wish to have your wrongs redressed, go out and burn ricks; government will yield nothing to justice, but a great deal to fear!".

Harriet, it seems, responded well to Lydia's appeal. In another letter to her dated December 7th, Lydia wrote:

I received a parcel this morning with the Cromarty post mark & *I think* in your hand-writing but without a line to say whence it came. Accept my thanks for the pretty things it contained. The little stockings were beautifully knitted . . . My box will I think be well filled. I & a little nursery maid I have got here have been making things *principally* to be given to the poor & I have got delightful contributions from friends in town . . .

However much Hugh's problems, and the antagonisms towards him they caused in parts of Edinburgh society, may have made their impact on Lydia, fundamentally her relations with Hugh remained sound. They and the children were together in Cromarty in October 1849. Their youngest child, 'little' Hugh, born 15 July 1850, was conceived then. Lydia wrote enthusiastically to Harriet Ross about him:

He is generally called as yet the flower of the flock as his little features are uncommonly perfect for those of an infant. I know you will join with me, dear, in praying that he may be the Lord's and that He would be pleased to accept of the little lamb as His own and fit him if He sees meet for His special services. The Lord's Providence has especially watched over him as yet. He narrowly escaped small-pox from the woman I had in mind for some time, attempting to conceal the illness of her own child of that most infectious disease, and we were directed in a most wonderful manner to a simple-hearted pious woman, the mother of a well-regulated family, and the wife of a worthy husband who makes a most admirable nurse.

Such pious hopes were usual in Victorian times; but it is interesting that Lydia had felt no need to include them when writing to her friend Jessy in Inverness (Chapter Eight) about her illness after Bessie's birth. Perhaps she felt them incumbent on her when writing to a former pupil.

But further problems followed. It may have been after the birth of Hugh that Lydia developed the 'spinal disease' which at her death was recorded as having been present 'for 26 years'. Although we do not know just what this 'disease' was, there is no doubt that at intervals after this time her mobility was sometime severely restricted. She also had continuing problems of other kinds. In a letter written probably about a year later she asked her mother whether she could 'call upon Simpson [presumably Professor J Y Simpson] to tell him ostensibly that I have been suffering so from diarrhoea that I fear I will have to give up the pills for some time at least *really* to see how matters stand in regard to the illness but this would need to be delicately done'.

These pills may have been calomel, known as 'blue pills' containing mercury, which were widely prescribed, as was laudanum. Over-use of both these drugs had serious side-effects.[36]

Despite her health problems, however, and the constant demands of domestic matters, Lydia found the time and energy between 1847 and 1856 to write seven more of her books for children. Time may partly have been available because Hugh, from the autumn of 1850 (when he spent some time exploring the 'wild districts of the western

---

36  It is interesting that recent research in the USA has led to the belief that use by Abraham Lincoln of 'blue mass' pills containing mercury was responsible for his 'uncontrollable rages' which ceased when he gave them up shortly after becoming President (*New Scientist* 21 July 2001).

coast' of Scotland), was busier than ever. Not only was he lecturing, editing, writing letters and reviews for other periodicals and travel- ling, but he was also busy preparing *My Schools and Schoolmasters* for publication in 1854, an instant success. He was nominated by Sir Roderick Murchison as secretary of the geological section of the British Association and a couple of years later he became President of Edinburgh's Royal Physical Society. He went as far as London in his lecturing, giving one to the YMCA in Exeter Hall with an audience of five thousand, and visited the Great Exhibition. He was also proposed by several eminent people, including Lord Dalhousie, for the Chair of Natural Sciences in the University of Edinburgh, which fell vacant in 1854. But the post went to a younger man, Edward Forbes, with an academic background. According to Bayne, 'it was the place which, of all others, Hugh Miller would have been gratified to fill'.

After searching for some time in company with his friend Maitland McGill Crichton for a new home, in April 1854 Hugh bought Shrub Mount, a substantial stone-built house in Portobello. In his *Annals of Duddingston and Portobello* (1898) William Baird wrote that it had probably been built by James Cunningham, Writer to the Signet, about 1787, and that 'though it stood close on the High Street it had then an air of comfort and retirement which made it an excellent family residence . . . and its well-stocked garden, which at one time extended to the sea, though in Miller's time only half the original size, gave ample recreation ground for the family'. This may have been one of Hugh's reasons for choosing it, although he was probably more interested in its position close to the shore and the space there was in the garden for erecting his private museum to house not only the finds of a lifetime but also 'new geological specimens which his researches in the neighbourhood were constantly bringing to light'. Here Hugh could arrange and catalogue his fossil fragments, study in peace and spend time with his own friends.

Lydia may have felt some reluctance to move even further out from the centre of Edinburgh and from many of her friends, especially as by then her spinal problem was making it increasingly difficult for her to get about. She often had to use a 'chaise' (wheel chair) and had to rely sometimes on others for help in finding and buying things she needed. For instance, she had to write to her mother to have a whole lot of plants sent (Lydia was a keen gardener), as well as clothes and other household necessities. Her thanks to her mother show how exacting she could be:

> The vests arrived and will do . . . There came likewise 2 night-gowns and fine chemises without either message or note. Now as I had asked you to get only two of the latter I thought they were sent on approval and kept *two*. I find however that you have paid five pounds. It will be necessary then to get either the other two or the money . . . I will be very happy to take the glass dishes if they are at all handsome . . . By the way would you enquire what kind of thin and loose shift is worn for girls' spring petticoats . . . woollen stripe like a fishwife's was the fashion through the winter. I never saw it but would fancy it too warm for this season . . . White slips would be such a constant plague when we are away in summer; if you hit on anything suitable buy enough for two petticoats one apiece for Harriet and Bessie . . . I would like also half a dozen small linen handker-chiefs for children at 2d each which you will easily find.

But life at Shrub Mount did have its compensations. One of these was having as near neighbours Lord and Lady Kinnaird,[37] who were very kind to her, particularly after Hugh's death. And the children must have been happy. Lydia's daughter Harriet, just before she died, wrote her last novel, *Sir Gilbert's Children*, which, according to her-self, was based on the family life there. It certainly includes details which fit with William Baird's description of the grounds, and of the adventure games they played which are also referred to by Baird (who took part in some of them). Although the background is roman-ticised (particularly in giving the father a knighthood), it is unlikely that she would have described the happy relations of the children with their parents as she did if she was not recalling her own experiences.

37 George William Fox, 9th Baron Kinnaird, 1807–1878, a Privy Councillor and later Lord-Lieutenant of Perthshire.

During a visit to Cromarty in the autumn of 1854 Hugh wrote a rather sad letter to Lydia: 'Cromarty is fast becoming a second 'Deserted Village,' and seems chiefly remarkable, at present, for its fallen houses and its vacant streets'. The shrubs and trees had been cut down, while 'the fine old woods and picturesque hedges are away'. Once again he had visited

> poor Eliza's little tomb-stone, half buried in long grass; I have looked out on the sea from the 'Broad Bank' and down upon the Drippping Cave and the Lover's Leap; and in looking back on more than twenty years when we used to meet, evening after evening among the trees, I felt how surely life is passing. It is now more than fifteen years since we buried Eliza. The hill is changed, like all else about Cromarty, and our haunt, right over the Doocot Cave, with its scattered beech-trees and its thick screen of tall firs, is now a bare, heathy slope, without shrub or tree.

He found too that one of his oldest friends was in a poor way. He told Lydia that he might try to offer him a loan. Lydia thought the loan had been applied for and evidently remonstrated. There followed the hint of what might have been a disagreement between them, for Hugh wrote back:

> I fear I must have sadly misled you by what I said regarding 'trying to lend – a score of pounds or so.' From your remark I infer that you think that he wished to borrow. No such thing. I have, since I wrote you, offered him the use of the sum proposed, and he has point-blank refused receiving it . . . We must not give things wrong names. There is not only *honesty* but high honour in such a determination; nay Christian principle of a consider-ably more genuine kind than that which leads so many vain Christians of the common type to come under unnecessary obligations to their neighbours. Possessed of the necessaries of life, they become beggars for the sake of its gentilities; beggars for the sake of unexceptionable bonnets and supernumerary frills, and the ability of playing Italian music on the piano; and fashionable saints charitably minister to their fashionable wants

by enabling them in pure charity to 'enjoy the vanities of life'. Depend on't there is an abyss of humbug in this direction.

If there was a hint in that remark of criticism of Lydia for a preoccupation with 'frills', it may have been partly justified. But her preoccupation was probably less to do with possessions than her own insecurity over money. She wanted her children to have the educational opportunities she herself had had; but above all she wanted financial security. If this letter was intended as criticism – and it may not have been – it was the only one in all the letters that have survived that could be thus interpreted. Hugh's letters to his wife, to the end of his life, were frank, detailed and affectionate.

And the end of his life was nearer than anyone realised.

# ELEVEN

# The Fall of the Oak

By 1856 Hugh was feeling, and showing, the effects of overwork and bouts of recurrent illness. Peter Bayne records in his *Life and Letters of Hugh Miller* that even the year before, when he saw Hugh for the last time, he had complained that his capacity for work was failing: 'He used to write an article at a sitting; he now liked to do it in two, relieving himself by a walk in the interval'. In addition to his editorials, he was trying to complete *Testimony of the Rocks* for the press: 'His activity had always been high-strung, but there was now a feverish intensity in his application which amazed and saddened Mrs Miller . . . He now moved restlessly about during the day, as if unable to concentrate his thoughts, and only as the darkness fell aroused his intellectual energies and compelled them to their task'. Reporting what Lydia had told him, he wrote that she would plead with him to rest but he refused to listen. Sometimes when she awoke in the morning, 'she heard, as she thought, the servants beginning their work, but found it was her husband leaving his'. She was afraid of apoplexy: 'The slightest noise distressed him . . . At night, before bidding him farewell, she would linger, on one pretence or another, trying to find an opportunity to remonstrate against his vigils, but she saw that he was nervously irritable, and she often feared to speak, lest the evil she wished to abate might be aggravated'.

During this last year of his life Hugh, normally a loving father, began to show signs of irritability with his children. But there were times when he could be his old genial self, particularly when there were visitors to Shrub Mount. One friend who had a talk with him on Thursday 18 December 1856, six days before his death, 'never enjoyed an interview more, or remembered him in a more genial mood', and 'on the Saturday following, another friend from Edinburgh found him in the same state'.

On Sunday he and Lydia went as usual to church in the morning. On the way home he remarked on the cold wind and asked if she would stay at home with him in the afternoon rather than return for the afternoon service as he did not feel well. Lydia agreed, adding that she too was very tired and that 'one of her limbs pained her'. She usually went to church in her chair, which Bayne called a 'basket phaeton', but had not used it that day. A few yards from Shrub Mount Lydia decided to call in on a neighbour who had had an accident a few days before, promising to stay only a few minutes, but Hugh was not happy to let her go.

During the time of the afternoon service 'he was in his most tender and confidential, which was always also his religious mood'. They had spoken only of religious matters and Lydia noticed yet another change in him which she had first observed in his prayers at family worship. In her own words, 'there was an increasing earnestness, a child-like humility, a more entire reliance upon the merits of the Saviour to blot out all sin, a more awful sense of God's immediate presence'. When he 'suddenly seized her hand, and kissed it with a manner she had never seen before' she was surprised at the intensity of his affection. 'There was in it a great deal more than affection, – an air of *courtliness*, so to speak, indescribable.' Afterwards she was to wonder if he were saying goodbye. She was sure that he dreaded the thought of 'some prostrating stroke, and that there were sensations in his brain which gave him the idea that it might be near'. She was right to think him afraid, but she had no idea that it was insanity he feared.

On Monday 22 December at breakfast Hugh told Lydia and his daughter Harriet that he had slept badly, a night haunted with dreams, and after breakfast, at which he had taken only a cup of tea, he announced: 'It was a strange night, there was something I didn't like. I shall just throw on my plaid, and step out to see Dr Balfour'. Again Lydia was surprised. During his whole life he had shown the utmost reluctance to take medical advice, and this was the first time she had ever known him speak of going voluntarily in quest of a doctor. But she encouraged him, so at about ten o'clock he called on their local practitioner.

Later Dr Balfour gave an account of Hugh's visit. On asking him what was the matter, he replied, 'My brain is giving way. I cannot put two thoughts together today: I have had a dreadful night of it: I cannot face another such: I was impressed with the idea that my museum was attacked by robbers, and that I had got up, put on my clothes, and gone out with a loaded pistol to shoot them'. He had then slept for a while but when he awoke in the morning he found himself 'trembling all over, and quite confused in my brain. On rising I felt as if a stiletto was suddenly, and as quickly as an electric shock, passed through my brain from front to back, and left a burning sensation on the top of my brain, just below the bone'. He had been so convinced that he had sleep-walked during the night, that he examined his trousers to see if they were wet or covered with mud, but could find none. The same feeling had affected him twice the previous week but he had found no evidence that he had been out in the night. He also told the doctor that while passing through the Exchange in Edinburgh the previous week he had been 'seized with such a giddiness that I staggered, and would, I think, have fallen, had I not gone into an entry, where I leaned against the wall and became quite unconscious for some seconds'.

Lydia was worried, and as soon as Hugh had left to see Dr Balfour she and Harriet decided to take the midday coach up to Town to call on Professor Miller. On his return from seeing Dr Balfour, Hugh decided to take the same coach for a reason of his own, and Lydia had to conceal from him their real purpose. When they got home, having arranged that Professor Miller and Dr Balfour would call at Shrub Mount next day, Hugh was already back and showed suspicion about their journey, which would have seemed to him an unnecessary strain on his wife's health. She had to confess the truth. Hugh at first was displeased but then agreed that Professor Miller might call on him next day. That morning, Tuesday, Hugh seemed better and managed to correct the last proofs of *Testimony of the Rocks.* Professor Miller and Dr Balfour called in the afternoon and found him still suffering from severe pains in the head and talking of the terrible nightmares he had been having in which he felt 'a sense of vague yet intense horror, with a conviction of being abroad in the night wind, and dragged through places as if by some invisible power . . . as if I had been ridden by a witch for fifty miles . . . ' The two doctors, after examining him carefully, concluded that he was suffering from 'an overworked mind, disordering his digestive organs, enervating his whole frame, and threatening serious head affection'. He was urged to let up on his work, go to bed early after a light supper and a warm sponging bath, and take a sleeping draught.

Harriet, who was still attending classes, had for her homework 'to produce verses upon given themes'. It was her custom to discuss the subject with her father, and after dinner later that day it was he who decided to read some Cowper, *To a Retired Cat*, which he 'read them with sprightly appreciation'. Lydia rose to make the tea. Hugh turned to another poem, *The Castaway*, which he began to read 'in tones of anguish'. This is a tragic poem written in a single day while Cowper was suffering appalling depression himself. In it he describes the last struggle of a drowning sailor – one of Anson's crew – and includes the words:

> No voice divine the storm allayed,
> No light propitious shone,
> When snatched from all effectual aid,
> We perished, each alone:
> But I beneath a rougher sea,
> And whelmed in deeper gulfs than he.

Lydia, reassured by the doctors' opinions, simply thought that Hugh was demonstrating to his children the contrast and range of Cowper's work, comic and tragic. Having completed the long and dismal poem, he then turned to *Lines to Mary*. This sentimental piece celebrates love between an elderly couple, and 'at certain of the verses, she could perceive half-stolen glances at her over the page'. Whether Lydia would have been happy to identify herself at forty-four with the 'wintry age' of the silver-locked Mary is doubtful, but maybe the following verse is the one she meant:

Such feebleness of limb thou prov'st,
That now, at every step thou mov'st
Upheld by two, yet still thou lov'st,
My Mary!

It had been an anxious two days and Lydia was exhausted. For some time now Hugh had been sleeping in a small room on the second floor next to his study because he thought the air there better for his coughing fits caused by his lung ailment. Lydia, however, to save her as much as possible from having to climb stairs, slept on the ground floor. After ordering Hugh's bath to be prepared in his study, Lydia went to her room and he to his study. He took his bath but not the sleeping draught. Some time in the early morning of Christmas Eve he rose, half-dressed himself in a thick woven seaman's jacket, went to his writing table in his study, took out a sheet of paper and wrote a final note:

Dearest Lydia,
My brain burns. I must have walked; and a fearful dream rises upon me. I cannot bear the horrible thought. God and Father of the Lord Jesus Christ, have mercy upon me. Dearest Lydia, dear children, farewell. My brain burns as the recollection grows. My dear, dear wife, farewell. Hugh Miller.

He then shot himself through the chest. He died instantly while the pistol fell into the bath. He was only fifty-four years old.

1. 'Hugh Miller's Grammar School, Cromarty'. Oil on wood painting
by John Muirhead RBA RSW (1863 to at least 1902). Presented by
him in 1885 to Lydia Davidson (daughter of Lydia Miller's daughter
Harriet, and later wife of Sir Thomas Middleton of Rosefarm,
Cromarty and grandmother of Marian McKenzie Johnston), then
staying in Cromarty.

2. Church Street, Cromarty, showing Hugh Miller Cottage and Miller House (with Braefoot Cottage). Oil on canvas, artist and date unknown – probably about 1880.

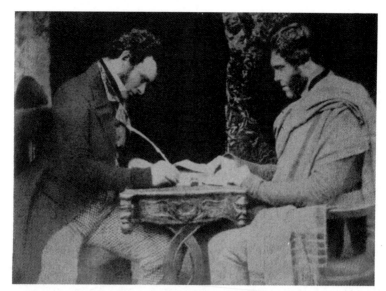

3. Hugh Miller, from a calotype by D.O. Hill taken between 1843 and 1847. His companion is John Robertson, possibly the Rev. John Robertson of Gartley, Presbytery of Strathbogie, Synod of Moray, who was ordained in 1819, 'came out' in the Disruption of 1843, and died in 1850.

4. The Millers' four children (L-R): Hugh aged 10, William aged 17, Bessie aged 15, and Harriet aged 20. From a photograph taken at Heidelberg during a family holiday in Germany in 1860. By kind permission of Inverness Museum and Art Gallery.

5. Egham Lodge, Surrey, from a watercolour of 1822. Lydia stayed here in 1829. By kind permission of the Trustees of Egham Museum.

6. Shrub Mount, the Miller home in Portobello from April 1854 to early 1857. A sketch from *Annals of Duddingston and Portobello* by William Baird (1898).

7. Loch Maree, visited by Lydia in 1862 on an outing from Poolewe. From a watercolour by Marian McKenzie Johnston.

8. The North Sutor, taken from the Gaelic Chapel in Cromarty in August 1867. From a pencil sketch by Lydia's daughter Harriet.

9. The Old Town of Cromarty from the Reed's Path below the South Sutor. From a watercolour by Marian McKenzie Johnston.

# TWELVE

# The Aftermath

It is not clear who first found Hugh dead, or when. Their close friend, the Reverend Dr Thomas Guthrie, in a 'memoir' written shortly before his death in 1873, describes hearing the news at the railway station on his 'return from a public dinner in Perth' and immediately hurrying to Shrub Mount. He learned only later that night from Hugh's half-brother, Andrew, that it could not have been an accident, as Lydia and others believed, but suicide. He believed that Hugh must have acted under the influence of insanity – while the balance of his mind was disturbed. He immediately realised that 'in justice both to him and to religion' and 'to remove the last lingering suspicion against Miller which the event might have raised, or his enemies been ready to take advantage of', there had to be a post-mortem examination of his brain. Next day, therefore, he returned to Shrub Mount and performed 'two very painful duties'. First, 'at the request of his eldest daughter, a very amiable as well as able young creature', to cut off a lock of Hugh's hair for her. Second to persuade a reluctant Lydia to agree to a post-mortem. To get this consent he 'had to undeceive her by producing that fond but fatal note which [Hugh] had left on his desk, addressed to her'. Guthrie wrote that he would 'never forget the face that looked up to mine, and the cry of agony with which the news was received'. The four doctors who carried out the post-mortem examination reported next day that 'from the diseased appearance found in the brain, taken in connection with the history of the case, we have no doubt that the act was suicide under the impulse of insanity'. Guthrie wrote: 'Having satisfied ourselves, we published documents which satisfied the public that Hugh Miller's reason had given way, and that he was in no respect responsible for the deed he had committed'.[38]

To have her husband declared insane must have been painful, but at least it removed some of the social stigma, and Lydia drew some comfort from realising that he had escaped either severe disability from the apoplectic stroke which she had feared, or incarceration in an asylum. A few lines written by her in a shaky hand, as a postscript to a letter from Harriet to Mrs Fraser, have survived:

> I write but a line to say how kind the Lord has been in these deep deep waters. *Every*thing that could alleviate the suffering of such a stroke has been given by His loving hand. Yet without that wonderful testimony of strong affection in that awful moment I know not how I could have stood. For that and the placid sweetness of the last few days, although that unconquerable will kept all its sufferings concealed, my soul will ever magnify the God of Salvation. How far otherwise it *might* have been under the influence of such a diseased brain!
>
> The sympathy is universal – extraordinary! Miss Borthwick has been more than a sister, but more than all other earthly comfort Harriet's fortitude, forethought, self control, and deep love and tenderness have been balm for the fearfully wounded spirit. She has been the wonder and admiration of all. My hand is not very well able to guide the pen.
>
> Great love and sympathy for the *mother*, my nearest fellow sufferer.                                        L. M.

The news broke three days later and shook Edinburgh. Public obituaries, reviews of his life and other testimonials filled the papers. Lydia received a flood of letters, some from the greatest figures in the land, including Charles Dickens, Thomas Carlyle and John Ruskin. The funeral, held on Monday 30 December, was one of the largest ever known. The cortège included the Lord Provost, some Members of Parliament, Free Church dignitaries and several thou-

---

38  This account by Dr Guthrie, included by his sons in the second volume of their life of their father published in 1875, differs in some respects from that given by Peter Bayne in *Life and Letters*, published in 1871.

sand citizens who walked the considerable length of a crowded Princes Street and beyond to the Grange cemetery where he was buried.

It was not just because Hugh had taken his own life that the crowds gathered under that dark December sky that hung 'like a pall' over the mourners. It was not just because Victorians were obsessed by the trappings of death, and appreciated nothing more than a good funeral. Hugh was genuinely admired for his writing. By many he was loved. As Michael Shortland put it when editing *Hugh Miller's Memoir*, 'Readers surely felt – one senses it to this day – that, with his latest volume in their laps, they had Hugh Miller looking over their shoulders. In choosing him, readers were choosing a friend'.

Lydia's postscript to Harriet's letter was a remarkable reaction, given the devastation she must have felt. That great tree to which she had clung as a girl and throughout her married life had suddenly fallen. 'If only . . . ' must have been two words that haunted her nights. If only she had been more patient. If only she had been more observant. If only she had been with him. How could he have brought himself to do such a thing? Why? How were she and the children to face the world without him? There would have been few to blame her if, as Queen Victoria did less than five years later on the death of Prince Albert, she had withdrawn into isolated mourning. But that was not her way. Her husband's reputation mattered to her more than her personal feelings. It must live on. Her first thought was to see that the printing of the *Testimony of the Rocks*, the proofs of which Hugh had finally approved just before his death, went ahead (it came out in March 1857); and she was able, with her knowledge of Hugh's intentions, to complete the revision of *The Old Red Sandstone*, first published in 1841, and see the 7th edition appear in April. But the effort, combined with anxieties over the welfare of the family, took its toll on her health.

By April 1857 a long rest, possibly a 'cure', had become necessary if she was not to suffer a breakdown. Perhaps her own doctor suggested Dr James Manby Gully's fashionable water-cure (hydropathy) in Malvern. But the suggestion more probably came from the Reverend William Samuel Symonds, the Anglican rector of Pendock in

Tewkesbury, near Malvern. He was an amateur geologist and natural historian who had greatly admired Hugh, and had given Lydia valuable help in the revision of *The Old Red Sandstone.*

It is impossible to be sure what income was available to Lydia and the children after Hugh's death (intestate). Apart from Shrub Mount (and a few other very small properties) to which William, as the 'heir male', became entitled on reaching the age of twenty-one, there was estate worth nearly £7,800 of which Lydia had a right to one third and the four children two thirds in equal shares. This included Hugh's half-interest in *The Witness* (nearly £4000), the copyright of his six books (one in the press), his private geological museum valued at £200 (and subsequently sold for £1025 to what are now the National Museums of Scotland), miscellaneous personal property and household possessions valued at less than £300, and £1900 in bank accounts. Lydia may have realised that with Hugh no longer at the helm *The Witness* might soon cease to be a reliable source of income. And indeed this turned out to be the case. It was put up for auction in 1864 at an 'upset price' of £500, but there were no takers and it was sold 'for an old song' to the *Daily Review,* its last appearance being on 27 February 1864. So if Lydia was anxious about the family's welfare, she had some justification for being so. Nevertheless, some surviving but incomplete accounts kept by the lawyers covering the first five years after Hugh's death show an income averaging about £800 a year.[39] Lydia may have had some income of her own arising from the nine books for children she had already published, and in 1857 she was awarded a yearly pension of seventy pounds by the Crown as the 'widow of the late Hugh Miller in consideration of services to literature and science'. (The Crown also, by the intervention of the Duke of Argyll, paid Hugh's mother

---

39 Direct comparison of monetary values in the 1850s with today without reference to different styles of living (and the differences in taxation levels) can be misleading. According to Bank of England official figures, £800 at that time was the equivalent of about £36,500 at the end of the year 2001. According to John Burnett's *A History of the Cost of Living* (1969), the writer Thomas Carlyle and his wife Jane (with one servant and no children) managed in London on an annual income of about £300.

a small pension.) So the family income appears to have been adequate to support a reasonably comfortable standard of living, even if it had to be carefully watched.

To put together a picture of the life of this bereaved family at this time is difficult. Apart from a few archival records such as sasines and census returns we have only a random collection of a few surviving family letters (mostly undated) and, for the first five years only, the incomplete accounts already mentioned. From the latter we can deduce that after Hugh's suicide his daughter Harriet (just seventeen) gave up her education at Mr Oliphant's school to devote herself to the care of her mother and the household; that William (aged fourteen) in January 1857 was at Mr Henderson's boarding school in Coldstream, some fifty miles south-east of Edinburgh, close to the border with England; that Bessie (in her twelfth year) became a boarder at Miss Mackenzie's school in Portobello; and that 'little' Hugh (six and a half) was taken by Lydia's mother, probably in April, to Cromarty and then over the water to board with Mrs Cameron, a relative of his father's, to attend Tain Academy. This left Lydia free to take Harriet with her to Malvern, probably by sea from Leith to London, where they stayed for a week 'of beautiful weather' with friends called Neville (perhaps connections of the Egham relations). The journey on from there involved three hours in a train to Birmingham, where they had to change to another going to Worcester, and then a coach to Malvern.

Despite the interval in London (or because of it?) the journey proved too much for Lydia. Writing to Mrs Fraser on 22 April from 'The Palms' in Great Malvern, Harriet said they had left London at noon and only reached Malvern at 8.00pm, Lydia finding the journey 'much more fatiguing' than travelling by sea. They went to an hotel for the first night, but then found 'such nice lodgings'. However, the weather had turned bad and Lydia had 'caught a slight influenza'. It was still out of season and they found that Dr Gully was away for a few days, so they could not immediately arrange treatment. Harriet hoped that her mother would have recovered before the treatment could begin and that they would be able to leave before the season proper got under way. But that was not to be.

According to Janet Browne, biographer of Charles Darwin, Gully's was one of two hydropathic establishments in Malvern, and at least twenty-four other similar places which had been set up in the United Kingdom by 1850. These were based on principles pioneered by Vincent Priessnitz at Graefenberg in Silesia. Gully had established his in 1842, and thousands of the famous, including Gladstone, Macaulay, Carlyle, Tennyson, Dickens, and even Florence Nightingale, were coming to Malvern each year to enjoy the benefits of this treatment. If, that is, 'enjoy' is the word to use. Darwin himself appears to have enjoyed Gully's treatment, using it five times, the last in 1850, but the regime was tough and did not suit Lydia.

Although intended to provide treatment for 'nervous' disorders as well as physical, such as dyspepsia, Gully's treatment was based on the idea that all chronic disorders were caused by a faulty supply of blood to the internal organs and that this could be corrected by a regime of cold showers and baths, wet-sheet packing and wrapping, steam baths, friction and rubbing, reinforced by a strict routine of early rising, walks on the Malvern Hills, a strict and plain diet, and spring water to drink (no alcohol or drugs). Practitioners were qualified medical doctors, but the idea was to allow 'patients' to have considerable personal control over their own treatment, according to what they felt they could and wished to endure. Indeed, the sudden spread of such establishments was partly the result of a change in the law which meant that people could no longer seek voluntary admission to asylums for treatment of nervous break-downs without being declared insane by two medical practitioners (a fact which became of some significance for Lydia a few years later).

We do not know how much of Gully's treatment Lydia was put through, or indeed how soon it was begun after 22 April, but in an undated letter written probably around mid-May (it mentions 'the smell of blossoming orchards') Harriet was telling Mrs Fraser that the treatment had had 'such an exciting effect upon [Lydia] that her nerves cannot stand it' and she was giving it up 'for the present at least'. And in a letter to Hugh's half-brother, Andrew Williamson, dated 16 July, Lydia herself referred to being 'again laid down with my spine' which 'is connected with the brain and I am susceptible to

the least fatigue and excitement . . . I am in the hands of quacks . . .'[40]
By 2 August Harriet was reporting that Lydia was 'improving. She is now able to walk from room to room without assistance, which is a great change for the better since it was only last week she had to be carried about'. But she was 'still far from strong' and Harriet thought it unlikely that she would be able to leave England next winter. By 16 August Lydia had ceased to be a patient of Dr Gully. 'After he had ordered her to be rubbed with oil and to lie a great deal in the open air he could do nothing more', wrote Harriet. So Lydia decided she could perfectly well do that 'without paying a guinea a week to him'.

There were various arrangements for accommodation while undergoing treatment. The most expensive was to stay in Gully's own establishment at a fee of between four and five guineas a week. For those who chose to live in lodgings the weekly fee was reduced to between two and three guineas (so Harriet's mention of one guinea is odd). In either case there was a charge of two guineas for the initial consultation. Lydia's address by then was 'St James', West Malvern, probably lodgings where a number of other patients were also living, for Harriet refers to its being too noisy for getting a good night's rest. So they moved to a small cottage nearby where Harriet rubbed her mother 'every morning with brandy and salt and at night with olive oil' which she thought was 'doing her good'.

What are we to make from all this of Lydia's state of health and mind at this time? Having wound up the spring of her nervous energy to see her through the three months of urgent work on her husband's papers and books, had the pressure been increased by the unsuitable treatment at Dr Gully's, leaving her again subject to physical exhaustion and an inability to walk? What in fact was wrong with her spine? In those days, indeed until quite recently, the medical advice to those suffering from back problems was usually to

---

40 It is interesting that by this time Dr Gully had already appeared as 'Dr Gullinson' in Charles Reade's (1814–1884) novel *It is never too late to mend,* published in 1856 and written to expose social abuses. Gully's reputation was finally damaged in 1876 by the 'Bravo' case, when his behaviour with the poisoned man's wife attracted strong censure.

rest, and there is evidence in letters and elsewhere that Lydia did often spend long periods in this way. This may simply have prolonged a condition that could have been improved with different treatment.

In her letter to Andrew Williamson she wrote: 'It grieves me deeply not to be able to get to Edinburgh where I feel my place is'; and she offered Andrew and his wife Maggie the use of Shrub Mount where she 'would not again reside if I went back to Edinburgh'. A reluctance to go back to Shrub Mount is understandable. But having fulfilled 'the melancholy duty of looking over [Hugh's] papers' (to quote from her note in the revised edition of *The Old Red Sandstone*), she was still determined to complete what she regarded as her 'sacred duty' to publish all Hugh's unpublished works and papers, which of course were in Edinburgh. The realisation of just how heavy a task this would be must have been preying on her mind and perhaps retarding a full recovery of her health. Help, however, was at hand where she was.

The Reverend William Symonds was not just rector of Pendock. Born in 1818 (six years after Lydia), son of the Lord of the Manor of Elsdon in Herefordshire, he was himself Lord of the Manor of Pendock and a Justice of the Peace. His church duties were light, leaving him time and energy to devote to local history, archaeology and geology. His interest in geology had begun in his youth and had led to his having contact with, and gaining the respect of, many eminent men of science, such as Charles Lyell, Roderick Murchison and Joseph Hooker. He had the knowledge of geology needed to understand and work on Hugh's papers, access to scientific journals and could correspond with experts in the field.[41] He and his wife Hyacinth must have realised Lydia's state of mind and persuaded her

41 Symonds was already President of the Malvern Naturalists' Field Club, which he had founded in 1853, and a Fellow of the Geological Society, and in his life he published forty-three scientific papers, mostly related to palaeontology. Of particular importance as regards his cooperation with Lydia at a time when Darwin's *The Origin of Species* was causing so much controversy, he was a churchman who believed that science helped in the interpretation of the Scriptures.

to stay with them while he helped her with her self-appointed task, in which he would have had just as much interest.

In the letter of dedication to Symonds included in the *Sketch-book of Popular Geology* (which was published in 1860) Lydia wrote: 'When my own overloaded brain refused to do its duty, you gave me to hope, by offers of well-timed assistance, that the task before me might still be accomplished. Your friendly voice, often heard in tones of sympathizing inquiry when I was unable to endure your own or any other human presence, – even that of my own dear child, – was for a time the only sound that brought to my heart any promise or cheer for the future. It was then, while unable to read the very characters in which they were written, that I put into your hands' the papers which contained the series of articles Hugh had written for *The Witness* about his geological 'rambles'. This led to the publication, with a Preface by Symonds dated 1 October 1857, of his edited version of Hugh's writings in a book entitled *The Cruise of the Betsey or a Summer Holiday in the Hebrides with Rambles of a Geologist.* This help from Symonds must have been an enormous relief to Lydia, especially when it became clear that she could continue to count on it while producing other posthumous works. The accounts show that she had a box, probably of papers, sent to him from Edinburgh in November.

With this support from Symonds and his wife, and the realisation that she was not alone in wanting to get Hugh's works published, Lydia recovered her spirits. Whether she continued to stay with them or moved into lodgings we do not know, but she quickly decided that she no longer needed to have Harriet constantly by her side and keep her from completing her education. In September 1857 both Bessie and Harriet entered a Miss Taylor's educational establishment in London. We know from the accounts that Bessie was in the Isle of Wight over Christmas and the New Year, and it seems safe to assume that Lydia and Harriet were there too.

Indeed Lydia may have decided to try further 'cures' in the Island (see Chapter Fourteen). There was a surgeon, Dr Samuel Weeding, practising as a hydropathist at 47 George Street, Ryde, and Lydia could have heard of him from someone at Malvern. She may have spent two or three months there. The winter climate was usually mild and it was a popular place 'for a change of air'. Lydia loved being on the sea or beside it and there is evidence that 'two boxes' were sent from Edinburgh to Seaview in February, probably containing papers requiring her attention in connection with further post-humous publication of Hugh's works. There was also a payment in March of an account rendered by a Mr Thurlow in Ryde, presumably Edward Thurlow who appears in *White's Directory* for 1859 under the heading of 'Watch and Clockmakers (jewellers etc)'.

Such evidence as is available suggests that Lydia's health was improving by the Spring of 1858. In April of that year arrangements were completed for the purchase of a house at 27 Ann Street in Edinburgh and Lydia must have moved into it in May, letting Shrub Mount (later sold in 1864 for £875). For the next five years she seems to have continued to have only occasional recurrences of her back trouble. She was able to enjoy family life and had the energy to be closely involved in the publication of five more of Hugh's post-humous works, writing prefaces to two of them. She also found time to write two more of her own books for children. She travelled, making two visits abroad, while also collaborating with Peter Bayne (who took over the editorship of *The Witness* for three years after Hugh's death) in his work of editing the essays Hugh had published in that paper, and the early stages of writing his biography of Hugh, eventually published in 1871 as *The Life and Letters of Hugh Miller.*

# THIRTEEN

# A Sacred Duty

Ann Street, on the other side of the Water of Leith from Moray Place, seems not to have suited Lydia (she had not herself seen it before purchase), for in 1860 she moved to 19 Regent Terrace (which she bought for £2100), selling Ann Street for £800. In the summer of that year she took the whole family for a holiday in Germany during which, on a cruise on the Rhine, they met twenty-six-year-old John Davidson from Burntisland in Fife, whom Harriet later married. In the spring of 1861, accompanied by Harriet, she spent a few weeks in Silloth on the southern bank of the Solway Firth, no doubt to enjoy the benefits of the warm sea-water baths. In August they both went to stay, probably as paying guests, with the Reverend James Noble and his wife at the Free Church manse near Poolewe on the west coast of Scotland. It must have been a comfort for Lydia, who seems to have been with them for the next ten months, to know that he had trained in medicine before training for the Church. Bessie was there part of the time, and certainly in May 1862 they were joined by young Hugh and Mrs Fraser.

References in letters show that Lydia had some periods of illness while there. Indeed in one letter Harriet says she had been 'very ill'; but she had recovered completely before leaving at the end of May 1862. In a letter to Bessie in London, Harriet described an expedition, in a party which included young Hugh, her mother, John Davidson (now officially engaged to Harriet), and Tommy Thomson, son of Hugh Miller's widowed half-sister. They 'went in a big boat with a sail' to Poolewe, from where they

walked about half a mile and got another boat in which we sailed up Loch Maree to the most beautiful little island I ever saw.

There we landed, and I'm sure you would have enjoyed wandering about under the beautiful green trees, and over the grass and wild flowers. I never saw so many flowers in one place before, the ground was perfectly blue with quantities of hyacinths and violets, and there were lots of primroses and little white anemones ... Then we sailed down the loch again and landed on some rocky bare island to look for sea-gulls' eggs. It was very nearly eleven o'clock at night before we got back ...

Shortly after this they left by boat for Glasgow, accompanied by John, and then overland to Edinburgh from where Harriet wrote to Bessie on 26 May that Lydia was 'able to go about the house just as usual'.

Only four months later, in September, Lydia, according to Harriet 'on a sudden impulse', took young Hugh on a trip by sea from Leith to Dunkirk, in France. On 14 April 1863 Harriet was married in Edinburgh, and she and her husband, now a Free Church probationer, moved to the manse at Beeswing, near Dumfries. At the end of May, or early June, Lydia returned to Silloth for two or three months, accompanied for at least some of the time by her mother and Bessie. For part of this time she was in poor health, but declined a pressing invitation to go and stay with and be cared for by Harriet and John Davidson, who were so near. Perhaps she did not want to be a burden on them so early in their marriage. Or perhaps she simply preferred to keep her independence when she was still attending to the editing of Hugh's posthumous publications.

How, in the midst of all this travelling and up-and-down health, did Lydia manage not only to write two of her own books for children but also to attend to the publication of so many of Hugh's posthumous works? These first five years of her widowhood show the strength of her character and her strong sense of duty inherited from her mother. In her preface dated November 1863 to the last of these posthumous works, *Edinburgh and its Neighbourhood*, she wrote: 'I have made it my sacred duty to give to the world, according to the repeatedly expressed intention of the author', manuscripts which her husband, because of 'pressure of work, an increasingly irritable brain, and severe attacks of inflammation of the lungs', had been unable to complete. But it was not only strength of character and a sense of duty that she displayed. She demonstrated too how right Hugh had been to see, more than twenty years earlier, that her mind 'was of no common order'. She corresponded with Symonds and others, and went through a mass of papers, to make sure she understood all the implications of Hugh's geological work and bring herself up to date with developments in the field of palaeontology. Her prefaces show how closely she must have followed and discussed Hugh's articles in *The Witness*. But they also show how fluent a writer she could be. She received a great deal of help from Symonds and others in preparing them, but the style is her own, not that of ghost-writers.

The first of her prefaces, to the *Sketch-book of Popular Geology* published in 1859, we can date from internal evidence to early October of that year. The book was a series of lectures delivered before the Philosophical Institution of Edinburgh. In her dedicatory letter she thanked Symonds for having given her 'all the advantages of your ready stores of information, both in carefully scrutinizing the text to see where any addition was required in the form of notes, and in referring me to the best authorities on every point regarding which I consulted you. And, while so doing, you have confirmed my own judgment, – perhaps too liable to be swayed by partiality, – by expressing your conviction that this work is calculated to advance the reputation of its author'.

Lydia opens her preface by declaring that Hugh himself had left the lectures in a 'shape perfectly readable' and remarks that 'every-one must be struck with the freshness, buoyancy and vigour displayed . . . ' She points out that the lectures were 'the spontaneous utterances of a mind set free from an occupation never very con-genial, – that of writing compulsory articles for a newspaper, – to find refreshment amid the familiar haunts in which it delighted, and to seize with a grasp, easy, yet powerful, on the recreation of a favourite science, as the artist seizes on the pencil from which he has been separated for a time, or the musician on some instrument much loved and long lost, which he well knows will, as it yields to him its old music, restore vigour and harmony to his entire being. My dear husband did, indeed, bring to his science all that fondness, while he found in it much of that kind of enjoyment, which we are wont to associate exclusively with the love of art'.

This is a well-chosen analogy and shows that Lydia understood at a deep level Hugh's passion for geology. She then goes on to explain why she believed it important to publish the lectures. 'They excited unusual interest, and awakened unusual attention, in a city where interest in scientific matters, and attendance upon lectures of a very superior order, are affairs of everyday occurrence. Rarely have I seen an audience so profoundly absorbed.' She explained that she had tried to persuade him to publish them in his lifetime but he had refused, seeing them as the core of a bigger project, a book on the geology of Scotland. That being no longer possible, she was publishing them in 'the hope that this work will be found useful in giving to elementary Geology a greater attractiveness in the eyes of the student than it has hitherto possessed'.

She points out that Hugh 'valued words, and even facts, as only subservient to the high powers of reason and imagination'. Too many books on science for schools were so ill-written and packed with ill-chosen information, 'that they are fitted to remind us of the dragons' teeth sown by Jason, which sprang up into armed men, – being much more likely to repel, than to allure into the temple of science'. Another good analogy, and here Lydia is recognising the importance of Hugh's contribution both to science and literature in his ability to write about the beauty and wonder of geological discovery in language that matched in style and elegance.

She then comments on 'what had been accomplished in geological research within the last two years' so that the reader will not feel that any facts have been repressed 'which clash with the theory of the succeeding Lectures, destroying their value and impairing their unity'. This was extremely important in view of the huge developments and changes in scientific thinking of the day. There were two schools of geology, she explains: 'the one, as expounded in the Lectures, delights in the unfolding of a great plan, having its original in the Divine Mind ... this may be said to be the true development hypothesis'. The other school believed that 'all things have been from the beginning as they are now . . . The next score of years will probably bring the matter to a pretty fair decision; for it seems impossible that, if so many able workers continue . . . in the same field, the remains of man and the higher mammals will not be found to be of all periods, if at all periods they existed . . . In the meantime, it is well to know the actual point to which discovery has conducted us; and this I have taken every pains [sic] most carefully to ascertain'.

But it is in her preface to the new edition of *Footprints of the Creator,* first published in 1849, that Lydia demonstrates just how comprehensive her study of geology and palaeontology had become. Hugh had begun to think about a revision, probably in about 1855, but, as she explains, 'he was not able to keep up with the demands of the time'. So, soon after completing *Sketch-book,* she set about it herself. Her research was formidable. Apart from getting advice from Symonds and Sir Roderick Murchison, she studied the work of such professors as Owen and Huxley, and scientists such as Louis Agassiz and Johannes Muller. She corresponded personally with Sir Philip Egerton, Professor Pander, the Reverend Hugh Mitchell of Craig, near Montrose, Mr Powrie of Reswallie, a fossil collector, and Charles Peach, 'that most invaluable pioneer of science'. But she also had to take account of Charles Darwin's *On the Origin of Species by Means of Natural Selection* which appeared in 1859 and sent huge ripples across the surface of much current scientific thought, as well as disturbing the equanimity of religious thinkers and believers. It was perhaps as much the latter aspect, as the pure science, that prompted Lydia, in her preface, to use her considerable powers of rhetoric and indignation to attempt to refute Darwin's arguments. Although, as Dr Mike Taylor, Curator of Vertebrate Palaeontology at the National Museums of Scotland, put it, 'her rhetoric was more impressive than her understanding of them', the quality of her writing is remarkable:

While we wish to speak of this work with the respect due to an accomplished naturalist, we must express our belief that it labours under two disadvantages. Its style is very much less lucid that that of *Vestiges (of the Natural History of Creation)*. . . and it likewise suffers from the want of implicit faith on the part of its author. This latter defect probably arises from the scientific character of his mind, which makes his theories, in so far as he ventures to carry them out, partly the result of personal investigations, and not altogether of hearsay evidence . . . Mr Darwin does not believe that all life has been developed from microscopic cells, – *that the fundamental form or organic being is a cell having new cells forming within itself*. . . The cell which contains the future oak, and that which contains the future human being, may be as essentially distinct in their kinds, and may no less require an intelligent deviser, and the forthputting of creative power, than the grown oak and mature human being. They are, if possible, more wonderful, as being more beyond imitation by any contrivance of art. By the creation of microscopic cells God may originate new species when it pleases Him, or, exceptionally, by the creation of full-grown individuals. The *fact* of creative power implies an absence of *limit* to creative power. . .

Was, then, this ancient repository of progenitive life, – this representative of chaos and old night, – filled only with strange rudimentary beings, framed after a pattern unknown to living nature, or to any of the successive geological epochs? Must our reason conquer imagination so far as to believe in this? Or may we not be permitted to ask if the mental process would not be exactly reversed? In order to be able to believe it, must not imagination have wholly conquered reason!

And were those odd uncomfortable creatures governed by *laws* different from those which have obtained ever since? For, otherwise, how could the *transmutation of species* be made more manifest in them than in those with which we are acquainted? . . . There is surely something egregiously false in a theory which has both to supplant real by supposititious facts, and to come into collision with that attribute of law without which man's reason would be useless and his researches vain.

Lydia ends this diatribe on a note of indignation:

> But the most efficient protest against this blind exclusive theory, which would inaugurate the reign of selfishness throughout nature, is to be found in the human heart. Childhood recognises a Father in Heaven in the daily blessings of its little life; and the more enlightened the mind unsophisticated by special theory becomes, the more is it brought into harmony with this first lesson of the heart. As the eyes of the understanding are opened day by day, the magnificent adaptations of Nature press forward evermore, as parts of 'one stupendous whole'.

She has used her formidable powers of argument in an attempt to counter those who wanted now to believe that evolution was not controlled by a deity. She was determined to keep God at the centre of His Creation. Those who believe that Hugh's suicide may have been caused by an inability to reconcile new scientific philosophy with his religious beliefs have missed the point. Hugh's faith in his own theories brought about by his own observations, echoed and understood by Lydia, was rockfast. Everyone else was mistaken. The present-day onlooker may see these beliefs as arrogant. They were not intended to be so. The nineteenth-century evangelical Christian believed and trusted with an unshakeable faith in the God of Genesis.

This edition of *Footprints* was published in 1861, but Lydia's undated preface must have been completed before she moved out of Ann Street into Regent Terrace in May 1860, for she could hardly have managed to write any of it while on holiday in Germany that summer. Perhaps, indeed, the holiday was a kind of reward to herself after getting off her chest something of which many must have heartily approved. Then, in addition to helping Peter Bayne in the selection of forty-six articles by Hugh, out of the more than a thousand he had written for *The Witness* over sixteen years, for publication as *Essays* in 1862, she was herself making her own selection for *Tales and Sketches,* published in 1863, of eight pieces from Hugh's writings in 'the first years of his married life, before he attempted to carry any part of the world on his shoulders in the shape of a public newspaper, and found it by no means a comfortable burden', as she put it in her preface, dated 23 December 1862.

Finally in 1863 she had 'the melancholy satisfaction of presenting to the reader the last of that series of works fit for publication left upon my hands by my beloved husband', *Edinburgh and its Neighbour-hood.* She added: 'If I am spared, and permitted health and strength sufficient for affording some little assistance in the preparation of a Memoir subsequent to [Hugh's] autobiography, I shall think that I have not lived these latter painful years quite in vain. At any rate, such materials as I have shall be placed in the hands of a literary gentleman whom I consider competent to the task', referring here to Peter Bayne, already at work on his two-volume biography of Hugh.

Once again, however, this great effort of will had taken its toll. Although the publishers dated this preface November 1863, she must have finished it earlier, for in October she had to be admitted to hospital to receive treatment for what appeared to be a nervous breakdown.

# FOURTEEN

# A Highly Nervous Organisation

None of Lydia's surviving letters mentions her own or Hugh's books. But doing 'justice to her husband's literary remains' was no easy task. Some of his posthumous works had already been published in *The Witness*. In a letter to Harriet Ross before Hugh's death, Lydia recommends one of his articles, but regrets she cannot send her their own copy as 'Mr Miller needs it', which may indicate that he kept aside those copies (editions) which he wished later to publish in book form. But the print was small, and some of his other works were still in manuscript. Hugh's writing was small, spiky and the lines cramped together. For someone with a 'weakness of the spine' and in the days before electricity, both print and handwriting were hard to decipher. And she had to deal not only with the editing and the prefaces, but proof-reading, publishers and copyrights.

There is a quotation from Henry Scott Holland frequently used at modern funerals: 'I have only slipped away into the next room'. Hugh continued for Lydia to be 'in the next room', if not in her head, until 1863 and perhaps beyond. Her grief at his death seems to have created the rush of adrenalin necessary to start on her self-imposed 'duty'. By April 1857 she was exhausted and hoped that in Malvern she would recover and be able to continue. With the help of Harriet and the Reverend Symonds her strength and determination did return, and she felt able not only to carry on with Hugh's works but to play her full part again in family life. However, by the end of 1863, with the last preface written, Nature took over.

Already on 28 May of that year she had written and signed a Will at Regent Terrace. She went to Harriet's and John's at Beeswing at some time in September, and there, on 3 October, she wrote a Codicil to that Will. She must have been displaying considerable emotional disturbance, perhaps talking of death, for Harriet and John to have become so concerned about her state of mind and behaviour that they sent for Mrs Fraser (now, be it noted, aged seventy-five). Together, probably also with the help of their own local doctor, they must have persuaded Lydia that she needed to go to hospital, for on 10 October she was admitted to the Crichton Royal Institution in Dumfries *voluntarily*.

As already mentioned, by that time it was no longer legally possible to be detained in such an asylum for treatment, even voluntarily, without being formally certified by two doctors as being 'a lunatic, or an insane person, or an idiot, or a person of unsound mind, and a proper person to be detained under Care and Treatment'. Admission as an 'emergency' was possible on the statement of a doctor, but within a maximum of three days a Sheriff had to authorise it. In this case the whole procedure was carried out on the day of admission and involved poor John Davidson in making a formal statement on a prepared form in which, in reply to printed questions, he declared that Lydia had been 'insane' for 'six days', that there had been 'frequent' previous attacks for which she had previously been treated at Malvern and the Isle of Wight, and that the 'supposed cause' of the present attack was 'family affliction'. The supporting statement by Dr John Dickson, of 20 Buccleuch Street, Dumfries, said that the patient was 'restless, abstracted and incapable of directing her attention. Fancies she hears the voice of her husband, who is dead, and of her daughter [Bessie] who is in Edinburgh. Has delusions of vision as well as hearing'. Stating what he had heard from 'her medical attendant and others', he wrote: 'Fancies that her food is poisoned; that she is at the point of death; and that she has committed the unpardonable sin and is given up to devils'. The supporting statement by Dr Stewart of the Crichton Institution was similar.

The Crichton was probably the best place Lydia could have gone for treatment. The Physician Superintendent at the time was Dr James Gilchrist, who may well have known Hugh, or at least his works. Born in 1813, he had begun to train for the ministry but had had to give it up on health grounds. He had then, at the age of thirty-three, turned to medicine, studying at Edinburgh and qualifying as

MD in 1850. But he was also a keen amateur student of Natural Science, particularly geology and mineralogy, and in *The Chronicle of Crichton Royal* published in 1940 it is stated that 'he continued its established methods of moral and humane treatment by means of occupations and recreations, specially, however, stressing the importance of the benefit of their educative value – by the giving of lectures on botany and geology and, with the aid of assistants and outside friends, on other branches of science, history and antiquities, and by the holding of field day demonstrations and excursions in the countryside around'.

There is no detailed record of what treatment Lydia received here, but such outdoor and mentally stimulating treatment, if she got it, would probably have done her more good than anything else. It was a charitable institution, catering for the poorest to the wealthiest. The annual charges for those paying when it opened in 1839 ranged from £10 to £350, with every patient having a private bedroom, its standard being progressively higher the more that was paid, going up to a 'Parlour and Bed-room' with private bathroom on the top scale, with 'wine, desert [sic] every day; game in season' and the 'use of a carriage or horse every day'. Lydia was paying at the rate of £100 per annum, which would have given her a 'Parlour and Bed-room' and she would have had her own table for meals 'with wine, desert [sic], etc three times a week' and the 'use of a carriage as an indulgence, a piano etc as a right'.

In the surviving case notes it is recorded on admission that she had a 'fear of self-destruction' and that she believed 'that her soul is lost'. They state that she had 'offered violence but with no malicious design apparently the result of morbid and blind impulse', and that 'for years back Mrs Miller has tried all sorts of quacks and has found no relief from their nostrums'. The next note was written on the day of her discharge, 13 November, and states that for five days she remained in a state of delirium and frenzy, that then 'by means of draughts some sleep was procured at night and from that date rapid amendment took place' so that 'in the course of the following week her friends who visited her declared her much better and nearly as well as before'. Mrs Fraser then rented a house in Dumfries and Lydia was discharged, 'so much health having been acquired in a short time'. The writer of the notes added: 'This case is an interesting one: a highly nervous organisation undergoes a perfect storm of excitement and delusion and in the course of a few days regains its balance. The only trace remaining is a condition of hypochondriasis which it is to be feared will never be eradicated'.

This contemporaneous diagnosis suggests that Hugh's early analysis of Lydia's temperament as 'a highly nervous one', and that her 'mind and body' were 'unequally matched' (Chapter Five), was shrewder than perhaps he realised. The report suggests that she may have been seeking medical 'cures' since 1857 more frequently than surviving papers show. But this does not mean that she was intrinsically psychotic or that her back problems were psychosomatic. It is quite possible that they, and her 'nervous' attacks, were the result of the medical treatment of those days, when what we would now regard as dangerous drugs, such as laudanum, were all too freely prescribed without proper supervision. Indeed, her recovery on this occasion, apparently within a matter of some three weeks, may have been as much the result of 'drying out' from such over-use of harmful drugs as of anything else. An additional strain on her 'organisation', of course, was the amount of effort she had been devoting to her husband's posthumous works. And here the mention of 'the unpardonable sin' and her belief that her soul was lost is significant. The 'unpardonable sin' was 'the sin against the Holy Ghost', which can be interpreted in various ways according to the translation and the Church concerned – not following one's conscience, despair, believing God has abandoned one. How much, one wonders, was Lydia in a religious turmoil as a result of trying to maintain her lifelong belief in the Creation and that everything, including Hugh's suicide, was God's will?

This was not the end of Lydia's 'nervous' collapses. She stayed on in Dumfries after being discharged from the Crichton, possibly encouraged to do so by Harriet and John, who would have wanted her to remain near them and to Gilchrist in case of any relapse. But how long she remained there is not known. She was certainly still there on 19 January 1864, when she signed an agreement on the security of

Regent Terrace (now let) in which the guardian of the orphaned children of the late Lieutenant-Colonel George Gordon of the East India Company's Bengal Army lent her £500. (This was a common way in those days of getting what amounted to a mortgage.) She probably spent at least part of the summer with the Davidsons, and may have been there for the birth of Harriet's first child, John Hugh, on 12 July. But she and her mother had by now decided to make a home together in Inverness, and the loan of £500 was probably for the purpose of buying Drummond House there. This had at one time been the property of her great-uncle, Phineas Macintosh, and before that of Frasers. Information in the records of sasines indicates that Lydia became the owner at some time during that summer of the house and something over two acres of ground. She and her mother were both definitely in Inverness shortly before John Davidson was translated that autumn to Langholm in Eskdale, some 15 miles north of Gretna on the English border.

Lydia was in Inverness over Christmas, with young Hugh (and a friend) and Bessie staying. It is not clear when Lydia first gave a home to Annie Thomson, daughter of Hugh's half-sister whose husband had died, who remained as her companion for most of the rest of her life. It seems, however, that early in 1865 Lydia may have had another 'nervous incident', leading her to seek another 'cure'. She thought of going back to Dr Gilchrist, but in an (undated) letter to her Harriet suggested a Dr Carruthers in Edinburgh, saying that this would be more comfortable than at Dr Gilchrist's, and that it would be 'quite out of the question that either Bessie or Annie could stay with you there. I think you ought to know that we were seriously alarmed about Annie: after your last illness she got into a highly nervous condition, and it would be very wrong to expose her to the risk of such a thing again'.

But Lydia, on whose advice we do not know but perhaps wanting to try other kinds of 'alternative medicine', decided to go to an establishment in Westmorland. She travelled to Langholm about the middle of May 1865, and from there Harriet, with her baby and Bessie, took her by train to Milnethorpe and stayed for a few days while Lydia settled in with a Mrs Jones. They were expecting her to spend several months undergoing some treatment, from whom is not known, involving rubbing her spine and, apparently, mesmerism. But Milnethorpe was another mistake. Lydia once again had a serious nervous breakdown and John Davidson had to collect her and have her admitted to the Glasgow Royal Asylum for Lunatics at Gartnavel on 20 June, at a rate of two guineas a week. Once again he had to go through the procedure of getting the Sheriff to authorise the asylum to receive her. Answering the standard questions, he stated that the length of time she had been 'insane' was 'under two months' and that the duration of the present attack had been 'a few days only', the 'supposed' cause being 'mesmerism and friction of her spine'. We have no details of what treatment she had been receiving at Milnethorpe, except the statement of the examining doctor at Gartnavel that she had had her spine rubbed 'with strong linaments' and had been allowed 'nothing to drink but strong hot porters'.

On admission, according to the medical notes, she was 'suicidal, having at one time swallowed a phial of laudanum and attempted to get out of a window [it is not clear when this was, or by whom it was reported], but is not dangerous to others. Prior to admission she was violent and incoherent and very noisy; and fancied the whole atmosphere was filled with divels [sic] ... On admission she is maniacally excited, screaming, struggling and kicking. She would not walk but had to be carried in and put to bed. After being put to bed she lay quietly and would give no reply to questions, but imitated the movements and repeated the words of those near her', a strong indication that she had indeed been under mesmerism. Clearly no voluntary admission on her part this time, and one wonders how John Davidson got her there. The diet of strong hot porters might have contributed to her condition. By the 23rd she was still 'dangerous and excited', but by the 26th she was 'out of bed, talks coherently, complains of great weakness in the back and feels much exhausted'. By 10 July she appeared 'to be very well mentally' but 'still complains of great weakness in her back'. She was discharged on 21 July.

During this time Mrs Fraser was living in Drummond House. In July 1865, while Lydia was at Gartnavel, Mrs Fraser consulted John

Davidson about the possibility of letting it, perhaps worried about having enough money for Lydia's expenses. John, on 7 July, advised strongly against this because 'our mother may be quite well in a few days or weeks, and may be wholly inclined to go to Drummond, and were she to find such decided steps taken, and to disapprove them, I very much fear it might induce a relapse. I cannot help thinking that she would feel very grievously hurt'. He recommended getting in touch with the lawyers in Edinburgh for help over money if necessary, and in fact in December, after Mrs Fraser had died, a further two and a half acres of land were bought with £400 provided by William 'of H. M. Indian Army'. Lydia had probably already told William (who may have been home on furlough from India at the time) that she would be leaving the property to him, as she did.

Mrs Fraser, who had asked Ellen Bayne to stay with her while Lydia was away, was not herself in the best of health, although no one, least of all she, seems to have realised that her trouble was serious. When she wrote (in an undated letter) to Bessie seeking news of Lydia at Milnethorpe, she referred to being very busy arranging new curtains for the drawing room at Drummond, coping with some troublesome sheep and calling on friends. But she died at Drummond on 18 August 1865 in the presence of Adam Bayne of Elgin, Ellen's brother, one of the Bayne family who had for so many generations been close friends of Mrs Fraser's family, who signed the death certificate. Also present was William A Campbell, surgeon, who certified the cause of death as 'Albuminuria, six months' (a kidney complaint). It is not known if Lydia was at Drummond at the time.

We have no record of Lydia's reactions to her mother's death. It is clear that Mrs Fraser had been a stalwart help to her in Cromarty, in Edinburgh and especially after Hugh's death, so she must have felt the loss deeply. Indeed the short obituary in the *Invergordon Times* of 30 August says Mrs Fraser left Cromarty 'some five years ago', which suggests that she may have made her home with her daughter in Edinburgh not long after Lydia moved into Regent Terrace in 1860, although still having the use of a home in Cromarty where we know she took grandchildren during school holidays. The first surviving letter after Mrs Fraser's death is from Harriet dated

9 September in which she says she is glad that Lydia was 'feeling somewhat stronger and more cheery'. She had young Hugh staying with her in Drummond House, and Harriet commented that he must make 'a good deal of extra cheerfulness about the house. Anything in the shape of a boy does that I think'. Indeed Lydia was feeling well enough to be urging Harriet to come and stay, as she had been ill; but Harriet, although tempted, decided they could not afford it, promising, however, to come the following summer.

Lydia seems to have been generally in good health from this time until late 1867, although evidently suffering bouts of back trouble. There is a remark in a letter to her from John Davidson dated 14 July 1866 that they were 'glad to hear of the new phase of your spinal ailment. I think it augurs great relief to you'. Harriet's second child, Lydia, was born on 15 July 1866. John had been able to arrange an exchange with George Mackay, Minister at Rafford and husband of Sophia, daughter of John Julius Wood, so they could afford to visit Lydia, with all three of their children and a nursemaid, in August. Later Harriet tried unsuccessfully to persuade her mother to leave Bessie and some friends in charge of Drummond and come herself to Langholm. But Lydia seems to have tired of being 'tied to Drummond', according to one of Harriet's letters, possibly also finding it too expensive. And in the summer of 1867, after much correspondence with Harriet, she decided to let it and return to Cromarty where she could live in one of the family homes there. How long she stayed is unknown. Harriet was there with her in August and probably Bessie too. Both Lydia and Bessie arrived at Langholm on 1 November from Edinburgh 'considerably exhausted' from their journey. In Edinburgh they had received hospitality from Robert Fairly. In a letter to him dated November 5th from Langholm thanking him for his kindness, Lydia wrote: 'I felt very sad as I entered the town. There seemed even a darker and heavier cloud over it than when I left it before from the death of some whom I had left in health and vigour. Yet I feel grateful to God for his goodness that he removed the misunderstanding between you and me so that I could once more go and see you'.

What this misunderstanding had been is not revealed. We can

deduce that since her discharge from Gartnavel in July 1865 Lydia had continued to have problems over the publication of Hugh's posthumous works, in which Harriet and John had tried to help. Among the remnants of correspondence from this period there are some letters from Harriet asking whether she and John could contact publishers for her, presumably in connection with further editions and the sale of copyrights. A particularly significant letter was written from Hull (where John was attending the opening of a new church) in July 1868. Harriet wrote: 'I don't know what Mr Burness [the Edinburgh lawyer] is doing now. We heard that the Blacks [Adam and Charles Black of Edinburgh were the publishers of some of Hugh's books] had refused to give more than £1500. I think the whole affair has been wretchedly mismanaged. And now I suppose the whole thing will slip through our fingers as *The Witness* did, and we'll get nothing'. Further letters show that similar problems were being experienced in 1869.

After Hugh's death the printing side of *The Witness* business, known as Miller & Fairly, continued to print Hugh's posthumous works for publishers until the business was sold 'for a song' in 1864. An edition of *Footprints of the Creator,* published by A & C Black in 1864, was printed by Ballantyne's. The 'misunderstanding' may have arisen over Fairly's part in arranging printing and publishing after the sale, and possibly even over his part in the negotiations for the sale. But it looks also as though the lawyers may have been incompetent, and perhaps Fairly had been able to demonstrate that no fault lay with him. It seems, however, that Lydia had found her continuing involvement in the printing and publication problems stressful. In addition, Christmas Eve must always have been a time of tension for her, and this year, the tenth anniversary of Hugh's suicide, particularly so. Whatever the reasons, she suffered another 'nervous prostration' on 28 December 1867 when John Davidson once more had to arrange her admission, under the now familiar emergency procedure, to the Crichton Institution. The case notes are brief, referring to 'great incoherence and occasional irritability: frequent mutterings and watchfulness with various morbid delusions . . . she says God told her to blow and was very angry if she did not do so. She would not keep her bed'. They give no indication of what treatment she received, but she was discharged on 1 May 1868. It is possible that by this time Dr Gilchrist, perhaps sympathetic towards this disturbed widow of someone whose works he admired, was encouraging her to let him keep an eye on her, for it seems she then stayed for a while in or near Dumfries, possibly with the Julius Woods, or perhaps in lodgings. She was certainly in Dumfries in November. We have evidence that she returned to Dumfries from time to time over the next few years, but there is no record of her ever again being an in-patient in any institution.

# FIFTEEN

# Lydia and her Children

Although there is nothing in surviving papers that can tell us directly how Lydia's children reacted to the death of their father or the nervous breakdowns suffered by their mother, such evidence as we have suggests that there was a fundamental family unity that gave them the strength to cope with the stresses.

To modern eyes Lydia may have seemed ruthless in abandoning her three youngest children so soon after their father's death, when she went to Malvern. But at that time, and indeed up until the Second World War, children frequently stayed for lengthy periods at boarding school or with relations while their parents were abroad or ill, or needed to 'get on with their writing'. Census returns for 1851 and 1861 show that Lydia too had young people to stay, for instance her young brother when he was a student, the Cameron cousins Margaret and Joanna, Ellen Bayne, a cousin of Peter's, Annie Thomson, Hugh's half-sister's daughter, Maggie Banks, possibly also a cousin, and her brother's two daughters.

It is not clear whether William, aged fourteen, was already at boarding school in Coldstream before his father's death or was sent there immediately after this. He may not have seen his mother again until the late summer of 1858, when she was back in Edinburgh. Entries in the account books point to his having spent his school holidays before then with his grandmother, Mrs Fraser, in Cromarty. He was sent in October of that year to a boarding school in Wimbledon and was probably back in Edinburgh for Christmas and New Year 1858. There was apparently a family holiday at Burntisland in Fife during at least part of the summer of 1859, the rest being spent again with Mrs Fraser in Cromarty. Both Bessie and William seem to have remained in London for Christmas 1859, but

William must have been back with his mother in Edinburgh for the first six weeks or so of 1860 (perhaps he was unwell), returning late to the Wimbledon school for the first term of the year. He was with his mother again in Edinburgh for the Easter holidays, and in the summer the whole family were together for the holiday in Germany.

Lydia would have been anxious to see him established in a good career. He may not have been particularly studious at school. In her letter written in July 1857 from Malvern to Andrew Williamson (Chapter Twelve) she expressed concern about William's academic progress: 'As it is necessary for William to pass his exam before the 15th it will of course be best for him to remain where he is for another twelvemonth. Mr Henderson seems to be doing him every justice . . . He has been pretty hard at work'. But we have no details of his educational achievements at Wimbledon. One of Harriet's closest friends was Jeannie Morison Buchanan, now married to Major (later Lieutenant Colonel) William Campbell of the Madras Regiment who was on furlough from India. It is more than probable that it was through him that William obtained entry to that regiment. He was gazetted Ensign on 4 February 1861, only three months into his 19th year, and left soon after for India.

We do not know how often he came home on furlough, and therefore how often Lydia saw him thereafter. But she did see him when he returned in 1872 to marry Maggie, the daughter of old family friends, the Reverend David Sutherland, then Free Church minister of the East Church in Inverness, and his wife Alicia Macdonald. But it was only a brief meeting in Dumfries, for she was not well enough to make the journey to Inverness for the wedding. William's military career, however, was a success. He rose to the rank of Lieutenant Colonel before retiring to Edinburgh and dying there in 1893. He and Maggie had three sons and four daughters. Of these only one daughter married.

*        *        *

Young Hugh was only six and a half when his father died. Even if he did not fully understand what had happened, the loss of his father, the turmoil in the household and the obvious distress of his mother must have affected him, and he must have felt Lydia's absence so soon after that even more deeply. But he would have received much affection from Mrs Fraser, who almost certainly came to stay at Shrub Mount, and no doubt went happily off with her to Cromarty before Lydia and Harriet went to Malvern in April 1857. He did not see his mother again until May 1858, when she came back to Edinburgh to live in the house in Ann Street.

So far as we know he remained with Lydia for most of the next five years. He may have been taught by her or had a governess until he went to Mr Carmichael's class at the Edinburgh Academy in the autumn of 1859. After the family holiday in the summer of 1860 in Germany he transferred to Edinburgh High School. (Lydia may have chosen her home in Regent Terrace specifically to be near this school.) The Census taken on 8 April 1861 shows that Mrs Fraser was staying at 19 Regent Terrace then, and it seems that she took Hugh with her to Cromarty for his school holidays while Lydia and Harriet went to Silloth.

We have no details of how the household at Regent Terrace was organised, but the Census shows that they also had staying there two daughters of Lydia's brother Thomas (at the time a Free Church minister in Singapore), Caroline aged eleven and Isabella aged eight (they may also have gone to Cromarty, but there is no mention of them anywhere in the surviving letters), and two sisters from Malvern as servants, Mary and Fanny Williams aged twenty-one and fourteen respectively. There was also a Margaret Banks aged fifteen, possibly a cousin of Lydia's husband, for whose education Lydia was paying. Although Hugh was with his mother at Poolewe in August 1861, he must have been part of that household in Edinburgh without her for the winter school terms. Lydia remained in Poolewe until May 1862, and Hugh may have joined her there over the Christmas and New Year holidays or gone to Cromarty.

Lydia's sea trip with Hugh from Leith to Dunkirk in September 1862 lasted a couple of weeks or so, and this may have been a crucial re-bonding. Lydia, as already mentioned, loved being on or near the sea and Hugh evidently shared this. Nine years later, after crossing the Channel to Calais, he wrote to his mother that 'the crossing in the steamer was rough but as usual I stood out among a host of folk gasping with sickness, as a monument of comfort, wrapping myself in my big Scotch plaid . . . chewing several lengthy sausages . . . '. But on return from the trip to Dunkirk there was another change in Hugh's education. He entered what the accounts referred to as the 'Queen Street Institute', which must have been the 'Edinburgh Institution for Classical, Mathematical, and Commercial Education' offering 'a thorough Classical and a high-class Commercial and Scientific System of Instruction for boys between ten and eighteen years of age'.

Such frequent changes of school may have been unsettling for Hugh. There is no information available about his academic progress at that or any other time, but another change was to come. In May 1863 he was sent to board with Mr Isaac Drape and his wife at the Green Row Academy in Silloth. This Academy had been founded by Isaac's grandfather in 1770 and by this time it was taking as many as 150 students from all parts of Britain, Europe and the West Indies. We have no information about what Hugh studied at this Academy. Harriet feared he was turning out irresponsible. But he was, after all, only fourteen. Lydia may have felt the same. She, accompanied by Bessie, was staying in Silloth for part of his first term there, and he spent the summer holidays of 1864 with her in Inverness. He was with Harriet (by now living at Langholm) for Christmas 1864 and had a friend with him, John Purves, son of the Minister at Jedburgh. Harriet found them rather boisterous. Writing on 31 December to Lydia, she said that the friend was 'away today, rather to our relief. Two schoolboys are rather a serious undertaking'. But she obviously realised that Hugh needed such companionship, for she added: 'There is a nice boy in Langholm . . . who will be a pleasant companion for Hugh'.

Harriet, however, wanted guidance from her mother in looking after her brother. He had received a letter from Lydia with which he was 'much pleased' when Harriet wrote to her mother on 2 January 1865: 'You say nothing of the *shooting* and we don't like to let him do it without your express permission. It would be well that he should know how to handle a gun, but of course there is always a risk of accident'. Perhaps Lydia, particularly at that time of year, had not felt up to agreeing that her son should handle what had caused her husband's death. But Lydia had also been advising Hugh on his studies, for Harriet added: 'I'm glad of what you say to him about his studies. John [her husband who had himself been a schoolmaster] says that *Chemistry* is of the greatest importance to him, and of that he knows nothing. Would you think of mentioning it when you write to Mr Drape?'

In the summer of that year, after Lydia had been treated in the Gartnavel Asylum (about which he may have known nothing), Hugh was again up north. Account entries point to his also visiting Tain and Nairn and going to at least one cattle show. He was with Lydia at Drummond for Christmas and the New Year with the additional company of two young Norwegians, Hans Peter Jenssen and his brother. Hans Peter was two years older than Hugh and they were the third generation of a successful Norwegian trading company. It is possible that they were students at the Green Row Academy with whom Hugh had become friendly (he stayed with them in France and Norway in later years). Lydia must have taken to them, for in a letter to her Harriet wrote: 'What particularly fine lads those Norse heroes must be'.

But Hugh seems to have been showing a disinclination for academic studies, as his father had at that age, and Lydia must have expressed concern at this in a letter to Harriet, who wrote to her early in January 1866: 'Have you made up your mind to anything about Hugh? It seems a difficult problem, and this time is so very valuable in his life it seems a thousand pities it should be wasted. Yet when I begin to speculate on what he can be put to I can come to no satisfactory conclusion.' It seems Hugh was being difficult with his mother (not unusual in a son of fifteen and a half), for in her next letter to Lydia dated 21 January Harriet was 'wondering what has vexed you so about Hugh.' Perhaps Hugh had been showing interest in farming as a career, for Harriet referred to a young farmer who had been one of their guests at a party for Bessie: 'The more I listen to his talk of his profession the more I feel convinced that Hugh is unfitted for it. It seems to need a great deal of activity, prudence and common sense, three qualities which I don't feel sure of Hugh's possessing. What I would fear most for him is the irresponsibility of it. An officer [presumably thinking of William] is responsible to his superiors as are most men to their employers. A farmer is at perfect liberty to squander his money, neglect his work, there is no one to find fault. I would be much afraid of Hugh's wasting his little capital and having to begin the world again penniless'.

Hugh's idea of farming, however, if he had ever seriously considered it, had evaporated by the autumn. Harriet and her children had been at Drummond House for several weeks during the summer, and Hugh had also been there after a term at Mr Drape's during which he had been receiving extra tuition in various subjects (unknown) including arithmetic. There must have been discussion at Drummond House about his future career, for Harriet, in a letter to Lydia written in September from Burntisland, where she had gone on with her children to stay with John's mother, refers to some plans for a banking career: 'I must say I thought Hugh's letter in some respects very sensible, that's to say that I do not see that Captain Graham's bank has any very great advantages over the Inverness banks, more especially if you could arrange so that he would not have to go back in the evening. Mr Ross's would have been a different thing, but I think that in Captain Graham's, more especially if he were there as a sort of supernumerary, he might probably only idle. How I do wish something could be found in Langholm. Tell me if you have said anything to him about the manufacturing business, and what he says to it'.

Poor Hugh! He must have found his mother's and sister's attempts to organise his life rather a trial. But nothing came of any of this either, because of Hugh's ill health. He may have been ill during the summer term at Mr Drape's (there is an account entry for 'doctor's attendance'), and he was certainly seriously ill next year, during the summer term of 1867, when he developed what was diagnosed as 'rheumatic gout' and had to be brought over to Langholm to be looked after for several months of pain and immobility. This seems to have been a deciding moment, although we do not know how the decision was reached that he should go to Edinburgh to begin geological studies. In 1868 he was in lodgings there, sharing with Norman Mackay, studying for the Free Church ministry, who subsequently married Bessie. He then went to the Royal School of Mines in London from October 1869 to June 1872, having been nominated by Roderick Murchison 'on account of his father's important contributions to the science of geology'. His career was at last decisively settled in 1874 when he joined the Geological Survey, and he eventually became Vice President of the Edinburgh Geological Society, after marrying in 1878 Harriet's close friend Jeannie, then the widow of William Campbell who had helped William to a military career. This marriage produced only one child, another Hugh.

Although Lydia did not live long enough to see Hugh married, she did at least have the satisfaction of knowing before she died that both her sons had embarked on respectable careers. She must have been particularly pleased that Hugh chose to follow in his father's footsteps (literally, in fact, nearly twenty years later when he undertook the formal geological survey of the Cromarty area): indeed it may have been her influence that was behind the decision in 1868 that he should do so. But both, Hugh in particular, may have been affected in some ways by the unpredictability at times of their mother's health and way of life, which did not always provide them with close maternal care. However, although so few of Lydia's own letters have survived, there is plenty of indirect evidence that she wrote to all her children frequently and was full of obvious love and concern for their welfare.

*   *   *

Harriet may occasionally have found her mother a little tiresome, but there can be no doubt about her genuine love and care for her. She became for a while the 'oak' to Lydia's 'myrtle'. At times Lydia was demanding, but she was also careful not to take Harriet for granted. When she was not in poor health or suffering one of her 'nervous prostrations', she was capable of being very independent. Her action in giving Harriet a chance to benefit from the stimulation and relative freedom of Miss Taylor's establishment in London as early as September 1857 was unselfish. She may have thought of the benefit she had received from her time with the Thomsons in Edinburgh when she was much the same age. More importantly she may even have realised that Harriet had been deeply affected by the events surrounding her father's death and hoped that by getting away from home for a while she might come to terms with them more easily.

We have no details of Harriet's life in London, but the accounts confirm what was written in her obituary in Australia that she had music (including guitar), art and riding lessons. Whether it was her own free decision to miss a couple of terms in 1858 in order to oversee the purchase of the house in Ann Street, Edinburgh and the move from Shrub Mount, or whether it was Lydia's particular wish, we do not know. Nor do we know whether the decision to finish at Miss Taylor's in the summer of 1859 was hers freely taken or another demand from Lydia. There is nothing in surviving letters to show how she occupied herself in Edinburgh from then on, but no doubt Lydia depended on her for the smooth running of the household, and the arrangements for the move to 11 Regent Terrace in May 1860, while she herself got on with the posthumous publication of Hugh's works. Lydia also needed her company for the stay in Silloth in the spring of 1861. But she must have been pleased by Harriet's choice of lover, and she seems to have done what she could to help the romance to fruition.

It is a pity that there are now no documents to show how Harriet and John Davidson, after meeting on the trip on the Rhine during the family holiday in Germany in the summer of 1860, kept in touch and decided they wanted to marry. John, born in 1834 and therefore five years older than Harriet, had studied at St Andrews and Edinburgh universities but had taken no degree. When they met in 1860 he was combining some school teaching with studying for the ministry in the Free Church. At some time in 1861 he became a licentiate preacher of the Presbytery of Kinross. After staying in Silloth for a few weeks in the Spring of that year, Lydia and Harriet went to Dumfries (probably to stay with their friends the Woods) where, according to a letter from Harriet to Bessie (in Edinburgh), John was going to meet them. For some reason he and Harriet felt the need to conceal their affair from the world at large, for Harriet asked Bessie to do them 'a great favour . . . We want to put the post office people at Lochend off the scent, so he means to address an envelope every day to Miss Miller at Edinburgh. It will be very funny and I want you to post one of the envelopes addressed to him every day. I will address and stamp them. If you have any letters to send to any of us you can just put them inside one of the envelopes. If you haven't, just fold a piece of blank paper and put it in. But be sure to post one every day and just open all the envelopes addressed to me in his hand, which of course you know . . . We'll likely put our letters inside his envelopes'.

It is not clear why such a subterfuge was necessary. But if John had been sent by the Kinross Presbytery to do some preaching at the Home Mission of Lochend under the Presbytery of Dumfries, he might not have wanted it known that he was addressing a Miss Miller only a few miles away in Dumfries. However, it is good to know that Harriet could indulge in such 'girlish secrets', and that Lydia must have been a willing party.

Convention, of course, would have ensured that Harriet and John could not have many private meetings (but perhaps Lydia, remembering her own trysts with Hugh, did not put excessive difficulties in the way). Later that year, however, Harriet, by now openly engaged to John and aged twenty-one, had a good ally in her friend Jeannie in Edinburgh. In December she was staying with Jeannie's family while her mother was with the Nobles at Poolewe over the winter. In a letter to a mutual school friend, Esther Ross Taylor, Jeannie wrote: 'You ask where Harriet is and what she is about. Well at present she is in Papa's study enjoying a *tete-a-tete* with the identical John Davidson of whom you speak! There are no *tete-a-tete* chairs in said study but there is a sofa which I rather think is considered preferable at the state of the business at which they have arrived . . . Her faithful swain has a preaching station in Fifeshire and of course yields to a certain magnetism which has the very frequent effect of drawing him over the water and leading him to turn up at 51 Lauriston Place. He is a rather nice fellow, rather nice looking and rather clever but nothing in a superlative degree. However he is Harriet's one idea and certainly fulfils the Bible injunction to "forget her father's house and brethren" . . . '.

He was indeed a 'rather nice person', particularly in the way he helped so much over Lydia's later troubles.

In 1861 the two Home Missions of Lochend and Newabbey in the Presbytery of Dumfries had been united under a single probationer Minister operating from the church at Lochend at the east end of the village of Beeswing some seven miles south-west of Dumfries. John had apparently been appointed to this post either at the end of 1862 or early in 1863, making it possible for him and Harriet to marry in April 1863. Harriet asked Dr James Buchanan, father of her friend Jeannie and now Professor at the new Free Church College, to give her away. He agreed, saying 'it would be an honour'. Life here had many pleasures for the newly married couple. In a letter to her mother in early summer 1863 Harriet referred to their having 'had such a charming sail on the loch', presumably Loch Arthur. John had to be away on church business from time to time, when Harriet could stay with the Woods in Dumfries. They were able to get away for sea bathing to Douglas Hall on the Solway coast. But they also had to cope with Lydia's nervous collapse involving her admission in October to the Crichton Institution (Chapter Fourteen). Although John was ordained minister on 17 March 1864 and translated to Langholm, they remained at Beeswing for the birth of Harriet's first child, John Hugh, on 14 July, only moving to Langholm in September. In 1870 John was translated to the Free Church in Adelaide, Australia, and the family left Scotland in early March. A fourth child, Harriet, was born there two years later.

*   *   *

Bessie seems to have been the least affected by the traumas of her father's death and her mother's breakdowns. She remained at the London school until Easter 1862, although apparently missing the summer term of 1860. Judging by the entries in the accounts, she probably stayed with the Nevilles in London for Easter 1858 and Christmas 1859, spending the summer holidays of 1858 in Cromarty and all the holidays of 1860 and 1861 with Lydia and the family, although leaving the Poolewe party in the summer of 1861 to spend some time with her Miller grandmother, Harriet Williamson, in Cromarty. On leaving Miss Taylor's, she remained for a time in London and was probably visiting various friends after this before once again going north, this time to Tain as well as Cromarty and Aberdeen. She was attending some unidentified classes in Edinburgh from October 1862. Account entries show that she was living most of the time in 1863 in Edinburgh, accompanying Lydia and Mrs Fraser to Silloth at the end of May but not to Harriet's in September, thus being spared the drama of Lydia's admission to the Crichton Institution from there. Again in 1864 she seems to have moved around between various friends (there is even an entry in 1864 for travelling expenses to Ireland).

Reading between such lines as are available, it seems that Bessie was something of a cheerful 'free spirit', disinclined to be tied to domesticity or her mother's side, perhaps understandable in a girl who became eighteen in June 1863 and knew that her sister was apparently willing to take on the responsibility of attending to Lydia's needs. Nevertheless she had no choice but to make her home basically with her mother in Inverness, staying from time to time with Harriet in Langholm helping with the children and the housekeeping. Harriet appreciated these visits and, no doubt recognising that Bessie was not getting as much young company as she should have, organised a party for her early in the new year of 1866 when, according to Harriet, 'she looked exceedingly nice in her white dress . . . as the guests were mostly young people we set to playing games immediately after tea . . . with great spirit'.

The previous year, as we have seen (Chapter Fourteen), Bessie had been involved in taking Lydia to Milnethorpe and was at Langholm when she had to be removed from there and admitted to Gartnavel Asylum, so for the first time she had personal experience of what her mother could be like when 'disturbed', perhaps her first real moment of maturity. She may also have been at Langholm when Lydia was admitted again to the Crichton Institution in December 1867: she had certainly been with her mother on their arrival there at the beginning of November from Edinburgh. She seems to have stayed with Harriet a great deal during the following two years, although possibly also at times with her mother, who was often living in Dumfries. Indeed she took refuge with Lydia at some time in late 1868, for there is a letter from Harriet to Lydia saying: 'I have written to Bessie asking her to come back. I am sorry we had a misunderstanding ... Meantime I can only ask you to believe me that as I don't lose my temper very often there really was some justification ...'. What the row was about and how long before this Bessie had left we do not know. Possibly she thought Bessie had 'interfered' with some of the housekeeping arrangements when, so far as we know, she was 'in charge' at Langholm during the summer when John, accompanied by Harriet, had gone to Hull for a couple of weeks in connection with the opening there of a new Free Church.

We do know from her letter that Harriet had 'been very ill for a week' in her very uncomfortable pregnancy with Jennie (born on 28 November), and Bessie had evidently returned to her soon after this because she wrote to Lydia from Langholm on 27 November. In this letter she waxed indignant over some 'mess' she found at Langholm caused, apparently, by a former servant whose 'carelessness amounted to wickedness'. Bessie had been 'up behind the ashpit, just to see if she had thrown anything out which she ought not' and found 'dishes *whole* without a crack or vestige of a damage half buried in the rubbish'. But Bessie was careful not to worry Harriet with all this and must have been a tower of strength at this difficult time for her. Harriet, however, seems to have had a somewhat elder sister attitude to Bessie, fond as she was of her. For instance, writing to Lydia after the party she had given for her in 1866, she said: 'Bessie has a great many curious theories, which you may have heard her propound occasionally, and John is very patient in arguing with her and often succeeds in bringing her round to sensible ways of thinking'.

Some time in 1869 Bessie seems to have moved to Edinburgh, but what she was doing there is not known. There are no further references to her being at Langholm or with Lydia, although it would be surprising if she had not returned to Langholm to give Harriet some help with her preparations for going to Australia. She was sufficiently fond of Harriet to lend her and John the not inconsiderable sum of £200 to help them with their initial expenses in Adelaide. By 1888 this had still been only partly repaid, although there were intermittent payments of interest. She married Norman Mackay, who while training for the ministry had shared accommodation in Edinburgh with her brother Hugh, on 2 July 1872 in Barrow-in-Furness. There were six children from this marriage.

\*     \*     \*

Although there is so little evidence to work on, we can see that Lydia's family had been able to cope well with her illnesses and breakdowns in her widowhood, thanks in large part to Harriet's having taken most of the burden of doing so on her shoulders in the early stages, and, later, to her husband's generous support. And from the tone of the surviving letters from her children it is evident that Lydia was always a devoted mother and grandmother, even if sometimes a little demanding. An example of this is to be found in a letter to her from Harriet written in the summer of 1868, when Lydia was living in Dumfries and kept on asking the pregnant Harriet to visit her there. Harriet, in a rare display of irritation, wrote: 'Indeed there is no chance of my being able to go to Dumfries. I would as soon think of flying as undertaking the journey just now. It is a very fatiguing one, there being four different changes on the way. Please don't urge me to come for I am really not able and it only pains me to be obliged to refuse so often'.

# SIXTEEN

# The Final Years

There is little material available from which to form a picture of Lydia's last years. When she bought Drummond House in Inverness and made it her home, shared with her mother, it looked as if she had decided to settle down in her birthplace. As we have seen, however, in 1867 she decided to let it. Whether she intended then to return permanently to Cromarty, where she went for a few months, we do not know, but there is no evidence that she went back there after leaving the Crichton Institution for the last time in May 1868. Nor do we know whether she ever returned to Drummond, although such evidence as we have suggests that she did not, unless perhaps to deal with tenancy problems. While she still had Harriet to visit and stay with, and while Bessie was still available to keep her company from time to time wherever she was, having no settled home may not have worried her. She had many friends with whom she could stay. And she still had intellectual occupations. She must have been corresponding with the publishers of her books for children over new editions of some of them, and also with Peter Bayne until at least 1870 on the biography of Hugh he was working on.

Although we have no record of her correspondence with Peter Bayne, it is clear that much of what he included must have come directly from Lydia. He had not himself known Hugh intimately. He had been chosen by Lydia to be Hugh's biographer partly because of the close association of his family with hers (see Chapter Five), but also because of his growing literary reputation. Born in 1830, Peter Bayne, who joined the Free Church, took his MA degree at Aberdeen University and then began to train for the ministry. But ill health caused him to turn to journalism and writing. For a short time he was editor of the *Glasgow Commonwealth* before taking over as editor of *The Witness* for three years on Hugh Miller's death. In 1860 he became editor of a weekly newspaper in London, *The Dial,* but this was a financial failure and Bayne lost all his own property and was crippled with debts for many years thereafter. From 1862 he was editor of the *Weekly Review,* the organ of the English Presbyterian Church, but resigned in 1865 because 'his views on inspiration were held to be unsound'. During the next twenty years he gained a high reputation with his leading articles in the *Christian World* and other writings, notably his biography of Martin Luther published in 1887. In 1879 Aberdeen conferred on him the degree of LL.D. His first wife, whom he married in 1858 and who bore him five children, died in childbirth in 1865. His second, whom he married in 1869, died in 1882 and his third became insane towards the end of 1895. He died a year later.

Bayne wrote that he had spent eleven years on Hugh's biography, and it is perhaps little wonder, in the light of his own family and financial troubles, that it took so long. Lydia's involvement in it was part of her mission to ensure that her husband's literary heritage was preserved and also a normal part in those Victorian days of producing in the form of a 'biography' what amounted to a funeral eulogy. This is not to say that Bayne did not conscientiously analyse Hugh's life, abilities and achievements. But he also included much of Lydia's (naturally partial) recollections and opinions. And he was persuaded to include one particularly unfortunate opinion of Lydia's which later had repercussions of some importance in assessing her own character. Bayne included Lydia's belief that Hugh's suicide could be blamed, at least partly, on his mother who, she believed, had so filled his childish mind with 'stories of fairies, witches, dreams, presentiments, ghosts' that 'the overpowering terror of those early times, the inability to distinguish between waking and sleeping visions, returned in his last days, stimulating the action of a diseased brain. The peculiarity of his mother's character told against him'.

We do not know whether Hugh's mother's second family reacted immediately to this when it appeared in print in 1871 (his mother had died in 1863), but it did not go unnoticed. Harriet Ross (Lydia's dear friend, now Harriet Ross Taylor) for one wrote in her *Recollections* that Lydia had been 'very misleading' in making these comments to Bayne 'which many had read with deep regret'. And some years later Hugh's half-brother's son, Hugh Miller Williamson, had his 'revenge' in an essay for which he won a prize while training for the ministry. This was never published, and had it remained 'hidden' no particular harm would have ensued. Lydia's descendants knew nothing of it until it was 'discovered' in the National Library of Scotland by Colin MacLean and used by him as a basis for his libretto for the opera by Reginald Barrett-Ayres, *Hugh Miller: An Opera in Two Acts*, performed at the Edinburgh Festival in 1974. In this Lydia was painted in a most unfavourable light, and others have since been influenced by the essay in their analyses of Lydia.

It has to be admitted that Lydia's comment included by Bayne was harsh and unbalanced. But Hugh Miller Williamson's 'revenge', in which he made her out to be a selfish, uncaring, hypochondriacal wife and a mercenary snob out to make money from her husband's death, was itself grossly unbalanced. He was born, in Edinburgh, in 1855, only a year before Hugh committed suicide and cannot, as an adult or even an intelligent youth, have known Lydia, who gave up living in Edinburgh in 1863. His essay was based solely on hearsay, partly from his parents and partly from (unnamed) 'relatives and friends of Hugh Miller, both in Edinburgh and Cromarty'. These could certainly not have included the likes of Robert Ross and his daughter Harriet, who were both alive when he was, he claimed, 'making careful enquiries'. He could possibly have gained the impression from his parents that Lydia was a 'snob'. We know from family members that Bessie told her children that Hugh's mother was not at first happy about her son's marriage to Lydia, whom she thought 'too grand'. However, we also know that Hugh's children stayed with her in Cromarty, particularly Bessie. Her granddaughter recalls the story that Bessie as a young child had been playing on the stairs of the cottage and asked Hugh's mother 'Who is the old man in the blue coat?' 'That', replied Hugh's mother, 'was your ancestor, John Feddes the buccaneer, whom your father saw when he was a young lad.' (See Hugh's report of this in his *Schools and Schoolmasters.*) But Hugh Miller Williamson's mother, Maggie, had been a 'servant in the

Manse' in Cromarty and Lydia had been an employer of servants. Maggie may have felt that Lydia had been 'snobbish' in her attitude to her. On what grounds Hugh Miller Williamson made other accus- ations against Lydia will never be known. He seems not to have been a likeable person. In 1992 a granddaughter of Harriet's living in Edinburgh remembered her mother speak of him. 'Och, he was a terrible trouble-maker in the family. He tried to stop my father marrying my mother because he wasn't good enough.' Who, then, was the 'snob'?

We do not know when Lydia gave Bayne her unfortunate opinion of Hugh's mother, whether early on in her widowhood or, perhaps more probably, much later when she was beginning to feel more lonely and maybe more bitter about the suicide. Harriet's departure for Australia in early March 1870 left her much more on her own. William was in India, Hugh studying in London and Bessie staying with friends all over the place (in December 1872 Harriet wrote to her: 'we never know where to address your letters to'). There is no telling how Lydia spent her time after this except that a letter from Harriet written from Australia on 17 June 1872 shows she was then in London, had been perhaps for several weeks (mail took six weeks each way) and was about to move on somewhere (Harriet addressed the letter to Dumfries 'not knowing where you are'). In London Lydia had been seeing Hugh and also Mrs Cameron, the relative with whom Hugh had stayed as a small boy in Tain. Harriet wrote: 'I almost wish you could see your way clear to staying there. Did you ever think how easy and comfortable it might be for you and Mrs Cameron to set up house together? . . . it would be a home for Hugh, which is a great matter'.

But Lydia was restless. We know that she was back in Dumfries in September of 1872 and that William stayed there a few days with her on his way to Inverness for his wedding. She may have been able to spend some time with Bessie both before and after her marriage to Norman Mackay in July 1872. But from some of Harriet's letters we can deduce that Norman was finding it difficult to get a steady job in the Church (he was not yet an ordained minister). Within a year they were thinking of emigrating to Canada, which met with Harriet's

approval. 'I think *anything* better than waiting on at Home', she
wrote on 25 March 1873, 'and the Colonies give such a much wider
field to a man's getting on, that I would never try to dissuade you
from going to them. I know I would not go back to Scotland now,
unless I had an Independence to live on. I consider the position of a
F.C. Minister there to be little better than genteel starvation. And
then the Church is so full of petty jealousies, bickering etc, that there
is little room for getting on in it. I wish you could come here, dearest
Bessie, but . . . all the good charges are filled up . . . '. So Lydia may
not have been able to count on much hospitality from them at that
time. They did, however, get a settled home in the manse at
Lochinver in the far north-west of Scotland, when Norman was
ordained in 1874 and given the parish of Assynt, and here they gave
Lydia a home at the end of her life.

Lydia did retain a close interest in family, friends and relations.
For instance she helped Mrs Cameron's two sons to go out to
Australia by lending her £20. But there are signs that she did not
really understand the details of her financial affairs. Correspondence between William and Hugh after her death shows that when
this sum was repaid she spent it on repairs at Drummond; but it
seems (although the details do not emerge from what has survived
of this correspondence) that it should have been returned to
William from whose account in Scotland it had apparently been
taken. And there are other indications that Lydia after 1867 had
become both preoccupied with and a little confused about her
property. In 1868 Lydia had correspondence with Harriet which
shows that she did not fully understand what possessions were in
fact hers to dispose of. There was some silver inherited from Mrs
Fraser which apparently Lydia wanted Harriet and Bessie to have.
As none of Lydia's letters about this has survived we do not know
precisely what she had proposed when Harriet wrote to her from
Langholm late in 1868 about arrangements for sending to her
things she had left there:

> . . . Then with regard to Grandmamma's silver. It is very kind of
> you to think of dividing it between Bessie and me, but it would be

hardly fair of us to take it while you are under an erroneous impression regarding Papa's silver. I have thought all along that you could not know how the matter really stood. One third of Papa's silver belongs to you to do as you please with, and leave to whomever you please. The other two thirds are in the same category as the rest of Papa's property and legally belong in equal shares to us four. If William had chosen the heritable property as his share *all* the silver would have belonged to him, but as he did not, but preferred throwing all into one stock, and receiving his share, the silver counts within the rest. Of course as long as you wish to keep it all in your own possession none of us would care to claim any portion of it; but Bessie and I don't like to take Grandmamma's from you, knowing as we do that we must come in for our share of the other afterwards.

This letter shows that even Harriet may not have properly understood all the details of the intestacy rules. But it also shows that Lydia's children were generously united in wanting to allow their mother to keep whatever she believed was hers so long as she was alive. They had even, it appears, raised no objection to her having disposed of some property such as books and furniture at Shrub Mount which were technically not hers to dispose of, although they may not have known about this at the time. The letter continues:

Papa's books belonged in the same way, which you evidently did not know, or you would not have parted with any of them. So I believe did the furniture of Shrub Mount. It is rather awkward for me to have to tell you this, as it seems like making a claim on you. I don't mean it for that, but only, as present circumstances are, I think it a pity that you should remain in the dark, because you might do things in your ignorance that you would feel vexed about if you knew.

What Lydia's reaction to this letter was we do not know, but there is no sign that it led to any argument or ill-feeling. However, her later testamentary dispositions left her family and executors with many problems.

The Will she had executed in Edinburgh in May 1863 was straight-forward enough. She left her mother an annuity of £20 per annum and the rest of her estate equally to her children on their reaching age twenty-one (which of course Harriet had already done) or failing them to their offspring. In October, just before her first admission to the Crichton Institution, she had added a Codicil bequeathing £500 for 'the support and maintenance of a female Bible reader' at the Canongate Free Church in Edinburgh; nineteen guineas to her maid, Bell Chisholm, and £10 to George Chisholm, shoemaker in Edinburgh; and to Caroline, the daughter of her brother Thomas, the £50 which Thomas had borrowed to set up house in Singapore in 1859. Thomas had tried to get Lydia to do even more for him, asking her to have his two daughters to stay with her in Edinburgh while at school there. In response Lydia pointed out that even were she to board them free, it would cost £80 a year to clothe and educate them, which she obviously expected him to pay. This caused Thomas to complain in a letter to his mother that this was two-thirds of many a Free Church Minister's income, and that 'according to Lydia's arithmetic I may say "Save me from my friends".'

Whether Lydia ever heard of this unkind reaction we do not know, but, as we have seen, the daughters did for a time become part of her household at Regent Terrace. As she had always been very fond of her brother, she may have relented and agreed to meet the costs; and the debt of £50 may have been repaid, for in a Codicil made at Langholm on 8 November 1867 Lydia cancelled the 1863 Codicil completely, made no mention of the £50 and otherwise simply reduced Bell Chisholm's legacy to £10.

Confusion was created when she executed another Will in Glasgow on 8 April 1875 stating that she was 'presently residing in South-ampton'. Why she was there we do not know. Possibly she had been having more 'cures' in the Isle of Wight. Nor do we know if she ever intended to return. It seems more likely that she was contemplating a return to live in Drummond House, and may have gone there from Glasgow. But by May she was at Lochinver, where she then remained with Bessie and Norman until her death the next year.

This Will, however, was a muddled document. It started by leaving 'the old house of Drummond and the land attached thereto' to her son William 'according to a will already made out and to be found in my small desk' (where this was is unknown), and to be 'burdened with the twenty pounds yearly therein mentioned to his sister Harriet'. This cannot have been the original Will of 1863 or any of the additions to it of which we have knowledge, for in none of those is there specific mention of Drummond or this charge on it. She went on: 'I wish three hundred pounds, there are already two, to be kept in the Chartered Bank of India and to be applied after a period of twenty-one years after my death in the following way ... '. The origin of this sum is not explained, and there is no other mention of it in surviving papers. The way it was to be used was extraordinary: 'with compound interest' it was 'to be applied to the benefit of that part of Inverness which lies beyond the river on the Tomnahurich side if possible in drainage according to the pneumatic system or a newer one if that will have been invented. The best way would be as it appears to me to purchase some of these neglected places which were heretofore to be got for no great sum ... and to improve them as circumstances permit'. Her two sons were 'to be combined in this Trust with Mr James Fraser civil engineer who has charge of my property'. At least, even if Lydia was showing a somewhat eccentric idea of what her money was to be spent on, it shows that she still retained some interest in scientific matters and in what was going on in Inverness.

The cottage which Lydia's mother had moved to in Cromarty after her husband's death was one of a pair, both of which it seems she had eventually owned before she moved to share Drummond House in Inverness with Lydia, who had in turn inherited them. Lydia now left them to Bessie, with the proviso that Annie Thomson should have the first five years' rent from them 'as a mark of her attentions to these my last years'. Only one of this pair, situated on the north-west side of the Court House, survives today. After Lydia's death Miller House, on the other side of the Court House, and Hugh's birthplace beyond that, Hugh Miller Cottage, became the property of her four children. Letters between William in India and his brother Hugh show that all agreed amicably that Hugh should look after them.

The Will disposed of 'that property in Bridge Street [Inverness] inherited by me from the Reverend Murdoch McKenzie Younger of Redcastle' to Hugh, 'burdened' with £15 annually to Bessie, and the wish was expressed that 'any of my descendants were in a position to repurchase the old Barony of Redcastle said to be the oldest in the North of Scotland and which belonged to the Mackenzies for many hundred years/my great grandfather'. The connection through her great grandfather, the Reverend Murdoch Mackenzie, with this ancient barony was a matter of constant pride to both Lydia and her mother; but whether Lydia really 'inherited' this property in Bridge Street as stated is not clear, although she certainly received rents from it. It is not certain that she owned, rather than received the rents of, 'the house next the front house and shop where the Reverend Murdoch Mackenzie lived, and rebuilt as at present by me', the rents from which she also wanted applied to the drainage scheme, with some very involved financial conditions.

This Will must have caused some concern to Bessie and Norman, as it certainly did to Hugh when he saw it; and it does not say much for the lawyers in Edinburgh, whose clerk, William Macdonald, actually wrote it out and had it witnessed by two 'warehousemen'. The document 'declares' that 'this deed was drawn by myself and merely extended on my behalf by the said W Macdonald', no doubt wording inserted at Mr Macdonald's insistence to show that he was simply carrying out Lydia's wishes in which he had been allowed no hand. In other words this Will did not have the benefit of any proper legal advice apart from getting it into a form which was expected to be legal. But on 29 October 1875 Lydia wrote a letter from Lochinver to an unnamed 'Dear Sir' in which she explained that Hugh was 'in a fright' about some 'Australian document of transfer'. What she was referring to is unknown, but she was anxious that 'if there is any flaw it must be rectified'. She was 'very low at present in bed and scarce able to speak' and was 'uneasy lest the Will be not siccar [certain]', asking for another to be sent for signature if the recipient of the letter agreed it was so. At the same time she wanted small changes to individual bequests.

It is not clear if Hugh had been at Lochinver and seen the Will there, or whether it had been sent to him to read. All we know about his contact with his mother at that time is from a cheerful letter he wrote her from Wark-on-Tyne (where he was on a geological survey) dated 28 January 1876 about a food parcel he was sending her. It contained amongst other things a 9lb leg of mutton, an 8lb shoulder of bacon, 14lbs of onions, and 7lbs of apples. In such an isolated place as Lochinver was in winter in those days, households would have had to rely for food on whatever they had managed to store in the autumn or whatever might, probably at rare intervals, come in by sea. The Mackays could not afford such luxuries as Hugh sent his mother, who in this way could repay them to some extent for their care of her – and no doubt ensure for herself a change from what otherwise may have been a frugal and monotonous winter diet. And this, we can deduce from Hugh's accompanying letter, was not the first or the last such gift.

But Lydia died soon after, on 11 March 1876, only a few weeks into her 64th year. No medical attendant was present, only her son-in-law, Bessie's husband, who signed the death certificate giving the cause of death as 'Disease of spine 24 years'. The funeral in Edinburgh on Monday 20 March, when she was buried beside Hugh in the Grange Cemetery, was not as great an occasion as Hugh's had been, though not bereft of mourners, even though it had had to be postponed from the previous Saturday as planned because of a snowstorm which had blocked the railway line from Inverness. It was not until 7 August 1877 that her sadly muddled testamentary wishes, from her first Will made in Edinburgh on 28 May 1863 to that last letter dated 29 October 1875, were finally 'proved' by the Sheriff of Ross, Cromarty and Sutherland in Dornoch and her trustees authorised to deal with her personal estate and effects 'in Scotland and England' valued at £793-15-6d. Even this figure had to be corrected later when it was found that it had wrongly included rents amounting to nearly £60 due after her death and therefore not forming part of her estate. History does not record how they and the family finally sorted out Lydia's wishes.

Harriet did not hear about her mother's death until May, only a week or so after John had heard of the death of his mother. Writing to

her sister-in-law, Maggie Davidson, Harriet said she was 'completely struck down. I was so utterly unprepared for it. My beloved
mother was by no means a very old person and I had always hoped
to see her again [the first time she managed to return home was not
till the following year] . . . For although she had long been an
invalid, one often sees those who are weak live on for years, while
the strong are cut down at a blow . . . It was strange that your
mother and mine should have gone so close together . . . Bessie says
that dear Mamma spoke so much of your mother at the last and
wished that she might go as gently. But alas it was not so, for she
suffered a great deal'.

\*        \*        \*

So ended a life of which twenty-five years had been spent in childhood
and happy girlhood, twenty as a wife and almost twenty as a widow.
Bessie later, after her sister Harriet's death in 1883, wrote in her
notebook: 'She and Mama have passed from our lives two of the most
mind, charm of presence and companionship I have ever met with and
cannot ever meet with in this world again, for combined with their
wonderful elevation of character and intelligent cultivation, there
was the closeness of our ties and the love of mother and sister'.
Bearing in mind that Lydia spent the last months of her life in
Bessie's home, and that Bessie must have known her well in sickness
and in health, this is a tribute not to be lightly disputed, even if it
cannot be regarded as an impartial judgement.

The well educated, intelligent, but somewhat naïve and impulsive
young girl who arrived in Cromarty in 1830 from Surrey turned into
the adoring and adored wife of an older man who, kind and gentle
though he was, was not always easy to live with. She showed her
mettle in Edinburgh, not allowing her own physical weaknesses to
affect Hugh's work or prevent her from herself becoming a writer.
Indeed, she helped eagerly with his work as editor of *The Witness.*
She also brought up a loving family of four children. It was clear that
after the tragic death of her husband by his own hand she had the
support not only of her mother and elder daughter, but also of a
great many friends who must have loved her. And her own strength

of character carried her through an experience which would have driven many a young wife into despair.

There was nothing lukewarm about Lydia. It was her enthusiastic nature that made her the good teacher in Cromarty that Harriet Ross and others adored. It was her dedication, and her strong sense of duty, that enabled her to ensure that Hugh's posthumous works saw the light of day, and that there were many distinguished people ready to help her in this. She never pretended to be a geologist herself. Clearly she had read Hugh's writings with understanding, and absorbed much of what she had overheard in his conversations with other geologists and in what he had himself told her over the years.

Above all, perhaps, we should note Lydia's sense of loyalty and her courage. Loyalty to her widowed mother in returning to Cromarty when she might have preferred to stay in the drawing rooms of Surrey; loyalty to her teaching profession through her school and her children's books; loyalty to Hugh in her unselfish love and, after his death, promotion of his works to the detriment of her own writing; loyalty to her children, all of whom were well placed in life and devoted to her. Courage in struggling against her physical ailments.

Exactly what Lydia's physical ailments were is unknown. She herself sometimes said they affected her brain and spine. Pain, of course, does affect the ability to concentrate on mental activity, and this may be all she meant. She may have been subject to migraines, and these can result from spinal and neck problems. Some of her descendants are afflicted with arthritis and osteoporosis, and these too could have produced Lydia's problems. But in the nineteenth century women's ailments tended to be attributed to 'nerves', and the medical treatment limited to 'a change of air', laudanum and calomel. The evidence of her admissions to asylums suggests that these were not the result of clinical mental breakdowns but rather of the effects of overwork and unsuitable use of drugs prescribed by doctors. She recovered from them with remarkable rapidity, and once she had finally completed her 'sacred duty', and had come to terms with what life had thrown at her, she never, so far as we can know, suffered in this way again. At the time of her 'breakdowns' Lydia was of the age when hormonal fluctuations can exacerbate emotional strain. It would be quite wrong to conclude that there was any intrinsic mental instability in Lydia's make-up, even if she occasionally displayed odd behaviour. On the contrary, what shows through is her intrinsic courage in coping with the many difficulties of her life.

This study of Lydia surely warrants the judgement that the wife of Hugh Miller of Cromarty was a remarkable woman, worthy in her own right of an honoured place in the history of nineteenth-century Scotland, worthy to be remembered alongside her illustrious husband as one who had helped him, as a wife, achieve his place in that history.

APPENDIX

# My Recollections of Hugh Miller
by Harriet M Taylor

(Copy of a surviving incomplete typed transcript of an original
which has been lost. The original, which was in the possession
of Bessie's daughter Harriet, must have been written after the
publication in 1871 of Peter Bayne's biography of Hugh Miller.
The writer was Lydia's former pupil and close friend, Harriet
Ross, who married John Taylor – see Chapter Five)

As I am, so far as I know, the only one now living who knew him well
it has occurred to me that I ought not to allow my pleasant memories
of him to be wholly lost. What he was as a literary and scientific man
is known to the world; but what he was as a man could only be
known to those who freely associated with him, and with whom he
was at perfect ease; and he was a man well worth knowing. From the
time I was but a child I saw him very often.. I shall speak of him as
*Mr* Miller for so I always addressed him and spoke of him; and to do
otherwise now would be a constant effort which it is unnecessary to
make.

My first recollection of him is seeing him in the Parish Churchyard bending over my mother's gravestone, hewing and lettering it;
which he was considered to do with great neatness. I was then seven
years old, and I used to play with my cousins in the 'brae' above their
father's garden, which adjoined the 'minister's brae' above the
churchyard. My sorrow at my mother's death was at the time
intense, yet soon I played heartily with my companions in this
favorite spot. Sometimes however, a sick feeling at my heart would
make me slip through the hedge which separated the two braes, and

I would go down nearer and nearer to Mr Miller as he worked. This at length came to be a daily occurrence for he in the gentlest, kindest manner encouraged it. While I stood beside him he spoke of many things, yet never seemed to be speaking *down* to the intelligence of the little child by his side. Graves were around us and some of them had been there for from two to three hundred years, so that the stones were sunk in the earth and covered with moss and lichen. I remember how he drew my attention to the first beginning of vegetable life on the smooth stone appearing to the naked eye simply as a grey stain; and how this decaying formed a soil for something more perfect; and he would tell me the names of the trees near us, bid me notice the different sorts of grasses etc. and so I was interested and cheered. And withal there was a thoughtful seriousness there among the remains of those who had once lived, some of them our own ancestors, and by the grave of her who had been so much to me. It was in September of that year or of the following one, he was still lettering stones in the churchyard, although my mother's was finished and set up, that talking with him there one day he said, 'I think of going this afternoon to the Doocot Cave. Would you care to come with me, you and your sister Mary and two of your cousins?' Of course I was delighted and so were they when I told them, and we joined him after school; Mary and I without dinner, and what was worse, without permission, either from our father or Betty, our nurse, whose rule over us was a very strict one. Mr Miller brought us with exceeding care down the steep side of the Sutor, and pro-vided with a light to show us the white-lined cave with its stalactites and stalagmites, and shouted that we might see the flocks of pigeons which made their home in the sides and roof of the cave; showed how his Uncle Sandy caught crabs, a difficult thing to do, and picked up and gave to us two lovely shells not to be found elsewhere in the district; for the living creatures to which they had once belonged had found a restful home in the quiet cove in the centre of which is the Doocot Cave. Both shells were univalve; one which clung limpet-like to the rock, but of a smooth shining black with dotted stripes of turquoise blue; the other whelk-shaped but coloured pink white and buff. Our enjoyment was great; but safely at the top of the rock there flashed upon me the startling thought that Betty would be very angry; and that Papa would hardly be pleased at our having gone without permission. Our kind friend had enjoyed so much liberty in his boyhood that the necessity for this had not occurred to him. We came off better than we expected, and never repeated the offence. And in truth my father greatly appreciated Mr Miller's kindness, and thought with truth that excursions with him were a great privilege and advantage for us. On many a bright Saturday he led us across the hill to sunny Navity where we looked out on the noble Moray Firth with its encircling mountains. At Eathie he shared our lunch by the waterfall. Ever as we passed along he drew our attention and interest to the objects around us – the sandstone rocks along the Navity shore, the Old Red fish-beds at Eathie, and what we admired more the Lias bed; for as he raised fold after fold of the thickly set layers ammonites, belemites and many shells, glittered like mother-of-pearl set in dark blue. Then there were the flowers, butterflies, moths etc. Those were happy days, and the memory of them is a happiness to me even now that I am old.

I am not sure when Mr Miller began to interest himself in what I read, and to lend me books; but it was from him I had an old copy of Robinson Cruesoe [sic], and I was about nine years old when he lent me Ivanhoe, and was amused at the extravagant delight with which I read it. It was only twitches of conscience which made me tear myself from it to prepare my school lessons. I well remember how kind his mother used to be when I went to return a book and carry away another and if her son was not within how faithfully she would deliver my message. She had a refined face and a superior cast about her, as all the Wrights had. She was most helpful to those around her in times of sickness or trial, and kind to poor people near her house, and in those days some old and feeble people were *very* poor indeed. I have been told by one who knew, that a few of these had a basin of gruel and oatcake by her kitchen fire every evening before retiring for the night. Old people have also told me how nobly she strove to support her three children when her husband in the ship of which he was master and owner, sunk at sea, and she was left very poor. I have written these things because of Mrs Miller's very misleading notice of her mother-in-law in Dr Bayne's memoir, which many read with deep regret.

To judge from what I saw of him in the earlier years of which I have been speaking, as well as at a later period, I do not think that he had any desire to occupy a different social position than that in which he was born; he had indeed ambition; but it was to be recognised as a man of intellect in the scientific and literary world. I think he was happy in those days; for his wants were few his time much at his own disposal, and he was greatly respected by all in his native town save those who disliked goodness, and they had felt his power more than once when they set themselves to oppose his minister – and his literary ability had by this time been acknowledged by good judges. But having become engaged to our highly gifted teacher, Miss Fraser, he was now anxious to be in a position to enable him to marry, and at one time thought of going to Canada; but life there would have ill suited the delicately nurtured girl whom he wished to make his wife. The engagement seriously displeased Mrs Fraser, her mother. The young couple were forbidden to meet in her house, so in the summer evenings we school-girls often saw them walking together on the wooded slopes of the Sutor – it was a favourite resort of ours, but as soon as we saw them we turned and went elsewhere. Miss Fraser was greatly looked up to by those she taught, and for myself in those days I almost worshipped her. Mr Miller has himself told us how he could at length indulge in the hope of being able to marry. After his return from Linlithgow, where he went for a year to learn something of banking he took his seat in my father's office, and then we saw him often to the great happiness of my sisters and myself. For my father and he became much attached to each other and were glad to enjoy a talk out of business hours and thus it was that, unless otherwise engaged, he had tea with us every evening. In those days and when alone we sat round the table; it was a light meal, not like the afternoon tea of to-day. Isabella was always sent to tell Mr Miller when tea was ready, and immediately he would appear with the little one mounted on his shoulder. The meal he and my father seated themselves on either side of the fire, Mary sat on her father's knee and Isa on Mr Miller's and I sat between them. Mr

Miller was the principal speaker but my father spoke too – he was a highly intelligent man and well read, especially in history ancient and modern; had a most retentive memory, and having been in the navy in early life had seen a good deal of the world. We were much interested in Mr Miller's account of all he had seen in Linlithgow; for indeed he had eyes to see both men and nature, and had observed more in one year, and in one small town, than many would have done in a journey round the world. Before leaving school on Friday Miss Fraser gave a subject on which each girl had to write, the paper to be given in on Monday morning; and I had a standing invitation to go to the office to show Mr Miller mine that he might comment upon it before I made a clear copy. I well remember how I went in very quietly, and sat silent by the fireside till his long column of figures was summed up, when he would turn round, and taking my paper, would read it with interest; and carefully point out to me where I might have done better. In the same way when I had finished a drawing I was never satisfied until he had examined it; I wonder at his kindness now. Mr Miller had a very correct eye, and gave a neatness and finish to anything he himself drew. When occasionally my father went from home Mr Miller slept in our house to safeguard the Bank money; and when he did so Betty allowed me to remain out of bed and sit at table with him while he partook of supper. On one of those evenings a large packet was brought to him, and opening it he said, "Those are the proofs of my 'Scenes and Legends' "; and picking out some leaves he handed them to me saying, "My dear, read that story; you may yet like to say that yours were the first eyes that saw my book in print." It was the story of Sandy Wright and the puir orphan. Near Mr Miller's home there was to be seen on all fine days a group of children at play and among them, the happiest and merriest of them all, a boy not like other boys – an idiot he was considered to be, Angus Mackay or Captain, as he liked to be called, the son of an old soldier who had seen much service. This poor boy was devotedly attached to Mr Miller and though he had never before moved many yards from his father's door, when Mr Miller came to the Bank, which was at the other end of our little door he at once followed him and soon made himself at home in my father's kitchen, and had his dinner there every day while my father lived. "Bless Miller, good boy! kind to me" was part of Captain's prayer before each meal. He was capable of the deepest attachment; and his love for what was good, and hatred for what was wrong and shrinking from bad company was assuredly heaven-taught. He lived to the age of sixty-three, kindly treated by everybody; and his mind seemed to expand as he grew older. Latterly he received a suit of clothes each year from the Poor Board, and it was carefully kept for Sunday until the next suit was given. In great business he was that day; and after my father's death came to my husband for his penny, and it must be a bright one, to put in the church plate. He went to the Free Church, and dearly loved Mr Elder who was for thirteen years its minister.

My sisters and I spent part of our holidays at the Hill Farm of Rariehig under Betty's care and before we left home Mr Miller wrote out for me a description of the obelisks in the churchyards of Nigg and Shandwick; bidding me observe them carefully; and also to be sure to go to see the fine caves of Carnuree which were of easy access from the hill. And when later on I went with my aunt to visit at Inverness he wrote to Mr George Anderson a lawyer then and a literary man, and a great friend of Mr Miller's, asking him to show me Craig Phodrig, and other objects of interest; which he most kindly did. Mr Miller was always so kind that I did not at the time realise *how* great was this kindness. How my sisters and I did enjoy an evening spent with him in his study as I may call it, in his Mother's house! The good women had laid out the tea-table and waited on us but did not partake of the meal. He treated her with the utmost respect and tenderness, and he was a prince in her eyes. We had tea out of cups brought from China by his father; and after tea he entertained us with tales, and choice pieces of poetry, some from Burns, and at length saw us home, carrying Isabella in his strong arms. But quickly the year /36 came to a close, and in January 1837 Mr Miller was married. This was a great event in the eyes of Miss Fraser's pupils, who all looked up to her and loved her; and now the school was to be broken up. It was the custom for bride and bridegroom, to have best man and best maid and when arrangements were being made Mr Miller said to my father, "John Swanston [sic] cannot at this season come from Fort William, and I will have no other to be my best man than this my dearest friend; but I should like Harriet to stand by my side and take off my glove." I well remember the gathering round Mrs Fraser's breakfast table on that bright winter morning; and then the assembling of the most respectable people of the place in the drawingroom; and of standing beside my kind friend. But when the time came to take off the glove alas! it would not come, for it was a tight fit and fully put on; but the bride's best man, he who was afterwards my husband, quickly and gently stepped forward and pulled it off. The newly married pair left immediately after the ceremony, as they had to reach Elgin, where was Mr Isaac Forsyth's home, before nightfall. When having bade adieu to all, and received the hearty expression of their good wishes, I standing well behind older people, heard the bride say "Where is Harriet? I must not go without saying good-bye to her!" and when on going forward she kissed me affectionately, I was a happy girl indeed.

After a few weeks, and when they were comfortably settled in the 'big house' which Mr Miller's father had built, my sisters and I and one or two other girls, went for four hours each day, save Saturday, to be taught by Mrs Miller; in this way she added a comfortable sum to their small income. Mr Miller generally returned from the Bank before we left. He came home by the shore; and on the beach, especially if it were ebb tide, he never failed to pick up something which interested him; and when he joined us explained what he knew or conjectured about it. And yet he had eaten nothing since breakfast time; but in truth dinner was not always in such a state of prepared-ness as might be desirable, for Mrs Miller had been occupied with her pupils, and the servant was careless. Most men would have been a little cross, but he most good-humouredly made jokes over failures and mistakes. I was a good deal with Mr and Mrs Miller in their early married life. "Come and take tea with us" was often said to me when school-hours were over, and I was well pleased to do this. Sometimes Mr Miller would sit and talk with his wife and with me; but oftener he wrote at a side table; and he always had a large Johnson's dictionary by him. There he wrote the Letter to Lord

Brougham, and Whiggism of the Old School, and many papers for Tales of the Borders. Mr Stewart said to me once, years after this time, "I never fully understood Hugh until he wrote that Letter to Lord Brougham. I never could get him to talk much to me; he always managed to make me launch forth on a subject on which he wished to have my opinion, while he listened intently saying aye! aye! every now and again: but I have long since learned to know and value him." On fine summer evenings Mr Miller took his wife out in a small boat which he had purchased, and in it sailed along the southern Sutor, and a little way into the open firth; and I was almost always with them. His step-father and the son of a cousin were the boat's crew. The former was rather talkative and not without some cleverness, but was what my father called 'a trifling body'; however he seemed most willing to serve his step-son, whom he treated with great respect. His wife married him, I have been told, because of his importunity at a time when she was oppressed with poverty, and thus incurred the deep displeasure of her brothers. We only went out on fine evenings, and as we kept as close as was safe to the shore we saw the rays of the westering sun clothing each outstanding rock and pinacle, and the trees in the hollows on the summit of the Sutor with a golden veil, while the opposite sides of these lay in deepest shadow – a poor description this of what was exquisite beauty, a beauty which caused a hush in the soul. Toward the end of the year a little daughter came to their home with wonderful eyes like her father's, she seemed to be observing and thinking all the time. Those who do not know say that all babies are alike; but this is very far from being true. This dear child lived for only seventeen months and latterly her life was a suffering one. Parting with her was a painful experience, and was deeply felt by both father and mother. The father carved the memorial stone in the garden behind his house, which was then a good sized and pleasant one, and it now stands where the cherished little one had been laid in the old burying ground of St Regulus. After my father married we sat in church in one of the three table seats, as they were called, in the gallery facing the pulpit; and in another of the three the Millers sat, thus I could not help noticing how intently he listened to Mr Stewart's wonderful sermons, sometimes leaning on the table with a hand on each side of his head as if to shut out the sight of everyone but of him who was speaking to us.

Towards the close of /39 a call came which could not be resisted to go to Edinburgh to help, as he was well able to do, in carrying on that great and important struggle which led to the Disruption. He waited till Mrs Miller had recovered from the severe illness which had followed the birth of a daughter, and then he went and took up vigorously the arduous duties which he had undertaken. Mrs Miller and her household were to follow him in April; and I had been so far from well during the winter that she most kindly proposed to my father and mother that I should accompany her in order to get good medical advice. This I did and remained with them till the end of July. We had a stormy passage to Granton so that the steamer which should have arrived there early on Saturday did not get into the harbour until daylight on that April evening had faded, and darkness had something [sic] set in. Mr Miller had been waiting for us since the morning, and must have been faint and weary though he did not show it but said he had been geologizing, and so had kept mind and body occupied. Sea-sickness had so prostrated me that I hardly remember how we got up to town; but we were set down at the east end of Prince's Street, in the midst of a crowd under the theatre which then stood there; and its glaring lights illuminated in weird fashion the faces of probably not the choicest class of citizens. But we did not stand long there but soon drove on by the Bridges to St Patrick's Square where Mr Miller lodged in the house of a young artist with whom his mother and the younger members of his family lived. It was a clever family struggling hard to earn a respectable livelihood, and sympathy with them had I think, much to do with Mr Miller's choice of lodging. Long and very wearisome was the ascent to it, being on the third, or I rather think the fourth story of the building. Mrs Miller had been expected to come early in the day, and that she would then arrange about the night accomodation of so large a party; and now at ten o'clock at night this was no easy matter; but we managed somehow till Monday when all were made more comfortable. The days which followed were fatiguing ones for Mrs

Miller for the house which had been taken in Sylvan Place must be furnished and she had to be out the livelong day making purchases. Her husband was too busy to help her, and even if he had leisure would not have been well suited to the task. In a few hours of leisure on a Wednesday afternoon he brought his wife and me to the Greyfriars Churchyard and as we entered pointed out the newly-made grave of Miss Fanny Allardyce, a Cromarty young lady who had been for a short time resident in Edinburgh; and he told us that a few weeks before he had met her in the street when she appeared to be in blooming health, and only a week after he was invited to attend her funeral. Her mother Mrs Allardyce, herself a gifted women, valued Mr Miller highly; and Miss Catherine, her youngest sister, was the close friend of both Mr and Mrs Miller – a person of singularly clear intellect, high-toned principle, and admirable good sense. The old churchyard for many reasons so full of interest I have visited again and again since then; and now there rests there the dust of one very dear to me. It was I think on the same afternoon he brought us to see a review of troops on Bruntsfield Links. What impressed me most was how those companies of strong men were swayed, and every muscle moved in obedience to one will. Ever since that day I have better understood when I read what forms alas so large a part of history, the marshalling of armies and the record of battles. I felt no stirring of enthusiasm because I was a girl, a lad would certainly have done so. The house in Sylvan Place was pleasantly situated; for from the windows in front we saw Arthur's Seat, and from the drawing-room windows an extent of the richly green meadows with fine trees here and there – much built upon now and different. Mrs Miller furnished the other rooms of the house, but did not find it convenient at that time to fit up the drawing-room suitably; a few things however were put into it and we found it a pleasant sitting-room. Books, which we had brought from Cromarty, and many new ones which came to Mr Miller as the editor of a newspaper were piled up around the walls; and at the foot of the room which was not a small one, his desk was placed. There he wrote all the long day and far into the night except on Wednesday and Saturday afternoons when he took long walks into the country. Mrs

Miller and I sat either working, reading, or writing, and took good care never to disturb him. He never sat, but walked up and down, repeating his sentences until they were moulded to his liking; occasionally coming up to his wife and saying, "Do you think this is the best way to put it?" and when satisfied went to his desk and wrote. At meals that on which he was writing was the subject of conversation, for we were generally alone and often a book was laid on the table out of which something was read. One day he said, "I am thankful to have my books; but" addressing his wife, "you know my dear, I took no books with me from home, and often during the past months I have quoted passages from various authors and in controversial articles on church questions and from books of law *entirely from memory*, and their correctness was never questioned." I liked to nurse the good humoured baby and sometimes when pacing up and down he would stop to caress it and more than once asked me if I thought she grew at all like her sister. There was a family likeness, nothing more. Harriet was the prettier child, and she was spared to grow up a pretty and clever woman; but there was a wonderful depth of expression in the baby Liza's face, and this child was soon taken where sin and sorrow are not. During night, although my room was not quite near the room in which he wrote, I could often hear him speak loudly as if arguing with an opponent. I have known him write continuously for eleven hours, and I heard him tell his wife that after writing many hours a pain seized him in one particular spot in his head on which he laid his finger, and she said, "O Hugh take care that you don't injure your brain." He replied "Dr Chalmers

(The typed transcript breaks off at this point, although it is clear that the original must have continued.)

# Bibliography

Allen, Margaret, 'The Author's Daughter, the Professor's Wife': Harriet Miller Davidson, *Journal of the Historical Society of South Australia*, No 27, 1999

Alston, D, *The Resolis Riot, 28th September 1843*, Courthouse Publications, Cromarty, 1993

Alston, D, *The Fallen Meteor: Hugh Miller and Local Tradition*, essay in *Hugh Miller and the Controversies of Victorian Science*, edited by M Shortland, Clarendon Press, Oxford, 1996

Anderson, I H, *Inverness before the Railways*, A & W Mackenzie, Inverness, 1885

Anderson, W S, *A Guide to the Free Church of Scotland College and Offices*, Knox Press, Edinburgh, 1994

Baird, W, *Annals of Duddingston and Portobello*, Andrew Elliot, Edinburgh, 1898

Bayne, P, *The Life and Letters of Hugh Miller* (2 vols), Strahan & Co, London, 1871

Browne, J, *Charles Darwin*, Jonathan Cape, London, 1995

Brown, S J & Fry, M (eds), *Scotland in the Age of the Disruption*, EUP, Edinburgh, 1993

Brown, S J, *Thomas Chalmers and the Godly Commonwealth of Scotland*, OUP, Oxford, 1982

Brown, T, *Annals of the Disruption*, MacNiven & Wallace, Edinburgh, 1890

Buchan, J & Adam Smith, G, *The Kirk in Scotland*, Hodder & Stoughton, London, 1930

Buchanan, R, *The Ten Years' Conflict*, Blackie & Son, Edinburgh, 1849

Cameron, G, *A History and Description of the Town of Inverness*, K Douglas & Co, 1847

*Centenary of Hugh Miller, being an Account of the Celebrations held at Cromarty on 22nd August, 1902*, Robert Maclehose, Glasgow

Davenport, L, 'Lydia Miller (1811–1876)', *The Edinburgh Geologist*, Spring, 1985

Davidson, Harriet Miller, *Christian Osborne's Friends*, W P Nimmo, Edinburgh, 1869

Davidson, Harriet Miller, *Sir Gilbert's Children*, published in weekly instalments in the *Adelaide Observer* from 22 June 1884

Delavault, P, *Pictures of Old Inverness*, Robert Carruthers & Son, Inverness, 1903

Dickson, N, *Cromarty: being a Tourist's Visit to the Birth-place of Hugh Miller*, T Murray & Sons, Glasgow, 1858

Elliston, A D, *The naturalist in Britain: a social history*, Allen Lane, London, 1976 (second edition with corrections and new preface, Princeton University Press, 1994)

Ewing, W (ed), *Annals of the Free Church of Scotland*, T & T Clark, Edinburgh, 1914

Fenyö, K, *Contempt, Sympathy and Romance: Lowland Perceptions of the Highlands and Clearances during the Famine Years 1845–1855*, Tuckwell Press, East Linton, 2000

Geikie, A, *Scottish Reminiscences*, James Maclehose, Glasgow, 1904

Gifford, D & MacMillan, D, *A History of Scottish Women's Writing*, EUP, Edinburgh, 1997

Gostwick, M, *The Legend of Hugh Miller*, Courthouse Publications, Cromarty, 1993

Grant, Anne of Laggan, *Letters from the Mountains*, Longman, Hurst, Rees & Orme, London, 1806

Grant, J, *Disruption Worthies of the Highlands: a Memorial of 1843*, Edinburgh, 1886

Guthrie, T, *Autobiography of Thomas Guthrie DD and memoir by his sons* (2 vols), W Ibster & Co, 1874/75

Hadden, J C, *George Thomson: the Friend of Burns,* J C Nimmo, London, 1898

Hall, N, *Travels in Scotland,* 1807

Hill, B, *The Remarkable World of Frances Barkley: 1769–1845,* Gray's Publishing Ltd, Sydney, British Colombia, undated

Jenkins, A & John, J (eds), *Re-reading Victorian Fiction,* Macmillan, Basingstoke, 2000

Kennedy, J, *The Apostle of the North: the Life and Labours of the Rev. Dr. John Macdonald,* T Nelson, London and Edinburgh, 1866

Kennedy, J, *The Days of the Fathers in Ross-shire,* Northern Chronicle Office, Edinburgh, 1861

Mackenzie, W M, *Hugh Miller: A Critical Study,* Hodder & Stoughton, London, 1905

MacLean, C, Libretto for *Hugh Miller: An Opera in Two Acts,* by R Barrett-Ayres, performed in Edinburgh 1947

Macleod, D, 'Hugh Miller, the Disruption and the Free Church of Scotland', in *Hugh Miller and the Controversies of Victorian Science,* edited by M Shortland, Clarendon Press, Oxford, 1996

Macleod, D, 'Hugh Miller's Prominent Role in the Disruption', *Ross-shire Journal,* 21 May 1993

Marshall, E, *The Black Isle: A Portrait of the Past,* J C Protheroe, Fortrose, 1973

Miller, Hugh, *My Schools and Schoolmasters,* Edinburgh, 1854

Miller, Hugh, works published posthumously by, and with Prefaces by, his widow, Lydia:

*The Old Red Sandstone* (revised, first published 1841), 1857

*Sketch-book of Popular Geology,* 1859

*Footprints of the Creator* (revised, first published 1849), 1861

*Tales and Sketches,* 1863

*Edinburgh and its Neighbourhood,* 1863

Miller, Hugh, Letters, notebooks, and manuscripts of and concerning Hugh Miller, geologist, National Library of Scotland, MS 7516-27 and Account Book MS 14248

Miller, Hugh, Letter-book (1825–39), New College (Edinburgh) Library (unpublished manuscript)

Miller, Lydia, *Passages in the Life of an English Heiress; or Recollections of Disruption Times in Scotland,* Richard Bentley, London, 1847 (published anonymously)

Miller, Lydia, books for children published under the name Mrs H Myrtle:

*A Story Book of the Seasons: Spring,* 1845

*A Story Book of the Seasons: Summer,* 1846

*A Story Book of Country Scenes,* 1846

*Little Amy's Birthday, and other tales,* 1846

*The Man of Snow, and other tales,* 1848

*The Pleasures of the Country: simple stories for young people,* 1851

*Home and its Pleasures: simple stories for young people,* 1852

*The Little Sister,* 1852

*A Day of Pleasure: a simple story for young children,* 1853

*Amusing Tales,* 1853

*The Water Lily,* 1854

*The Ocean Child: or, Showers and Sunshine. A tale of girlhood,* 1857

*Always do your best, and Lizzie Lindsay,* 1859

*A visit to the New Forest: a tale,* 1859

*Aunt Maddy's Diamonds. A tale for little girls,* 1864

*Country Scenes, and tales of the four seasons,* 1866

Miller, Lydia, *Cats and Dogs, Nature's Warriors and God's Workers: or Mrs Myrtle's Lessons in natural History,* 1857 (published under initials L F F M)

Miller, Lydia, 'Journal', edited and published by her granddaughter Lydia Miller Mackay in *Chambers' Journal,* VIth series, April–July 1902

Noble, J, *Religious Life in Ross,* J Thin, Edinburgh, 1909

Rosie, G, *Hugh Miller: Outrage and Order: A Biography and Selected Writings,* Mainstream Publishing, Edinburgh, 1981

Sage, D (ed by his son D F Sage), *Memorabilia Domestica or Parish Life in the North of Scotland*, W Rae, Wick, 1889 and 1899

Scott, Hew, *Fasti Ecclesiæ Scoticanæ*, Oliver & Boyd, Edinburgh, 1926–28

Shortland, M (ed), *Hugh Miller's Memoir: From Stonemason to Geologist*, EUP, Edinburgh, 1995

Stevenson, S F, 'Drawing the Crowd: an Approach to Democracy in the Calotypes of D O Hill and Robert Adamson', *Scotland's Journal*, 1996

Suter, J, *Memorabilia of Inverness*, Donald Macdonald, Inverness, 1887

Sutherland, E, *Ravens and Black Rain*, Constable, London, 1985

Taylor, M, 'Hugh Miller and his Fossils', *The Edinburgh Geologist*, Spring 2002

Warr, C L, *The Presbyterian Tradition*, Alexander Maclehose & Co, Glasgow, 1930

Waterston, C D, *Hugh Miller: The Cromarty Stonemason*, National Trust for Scotland, Edinburgh, 1966

Williamson, H M, Essay on the Life of Hugh Miller, unpublished manuscript, National Library of Scotland, MS 7527, 1881

Willis, D P, *Discovering the Black Isle*, John Donald, Edinburgh, 1989

# Index